More

Grandmother's Prayers

---

60 DAYS OF
DEVOTIONS AND PRAYER

Kay Swatkowski

Our Daily Bread
Publishing™

Requests for permission to quote from this book should be directed to: Permissions Department, Our Daily Bread Publishing, PO Box 3566, Grand Rapids, MI 49501, or contact us by email at permissionsdept@odb.org.

Scripture quotations, unless otherwise indicated, are taken from the ESV® Bible (The Holy Bible, English Standard Version®), copyright © 2001 by Crossway, a publishing ministry of Good News Publishers. Used by permission. All rights reserved.

Scripture quotations marked HCSB are from the Holman Christian Standard Bible®. Copyright © 1999, 2000, 2002, 2003, 2009 by Holman Bible Publishers. Used by permission. Holman Christian Standard Bible®, Holman CSB®, and HCSB® are federally registered trademarks of Holman Bible Publishers.

Scripture quotations marked NIV are taken from the Holy Bible, New International Version®, NIV®. Copyright © 1973, 1978, 1984, 2011 by Biblica, Inc.™ Used by permission of Zondervan. All rights reserved worldwide. www.zondervan.com.

Scripture quotations marked NLT are taken from the Holy Bible, New Living Translation, copyright © 1996, 2004, 2015 by Tyndale House Foundation. Used by permission of Tyndale House Publishers, Inc., Carol Stream, Illinois 60188. All rights reserved.

Scripture quotations marked WEB are from the World English Bible (WEB). Public domain.

Library of Congress Cataloging-in-Publication Data
Names: Swatkowski, Kay, author.
Title: More grandmother's prayers : 60 days of devotions and prayer / Kay Swatkowski.
Description: Grand Rapids, MI : Our Daily Bread Publishing, [2022] | Summary: "Grandmothers will find encouragement and biblical guidance in how to pray for and meaningfully interact with their grandchildren through 60 days of devotions"-- Provided by publisher.
Identifiers: LCCN 2021055903 | ISBN 9781640701632
Subjects: LCSH: Grandmothers--Prayers and devotions. | BISAC: RELIGION / Christian Living / Prayer | FAMILY & RELATIONSHIPS / Parenting / Grandparenting
Classification: LCC BV4847 .S845 2022 | DDC 242/.6431--dc23/eng/20220128
LC record available at https://lccn.loc.gov/2021055903

Printed in the United States of America

22 23 24 25 26 27 28 29 / 8 7 6 5 4 3 2 1

In loving memory of our dear friend,
who faithfully lifted our family up in prayer.
Thomas Volney Good
1946–2016

Contents

Acknowledgments

First, thank you to my loving and supportive husband, Ray. Without your constant encouragement and help, this book would still be an idea sitting on my desk. Thank you for the meals, laundry, shopping, and a thousand other tasks that you shouldered so I could devote myself to this work. I am grateful for the life and ministry we share.

Thank you to our children for always being my cheerleaders. Jennifer, Jonathan, Lindy, Julie, Justin, Joy, and Tim, we are so proud of you all. We thank the Lord for each of you.

Thank you to all our grandchildren. Nicole, Kevin, Samantha, Madelyn, Holden, Aiden, Noah, Avett, and Xavier. You are the inspiration for this book. Thank you for your laughter and love. You have made our lives full and fascinating. You are always in my prayers.

Thank you to my friend Cheryl Tanner. Always ready to discuss ideas and share your thoughts, you helped me to find new gems in God's Word. Your fresh insights and sincere love for God always propelled me forward. I am blessed to have such a friend.

Thank you to my sisters, Susan, Lisa, and Erin. Your interest and patience mean so much. Your love for your grandchildren always reminds me how important it is for grandmothers to pray.

A sincere thank you to our friends at Our Daily Bread Publishing. Thank you to Dawn Anderson for opening the door to this project. Your patience and help were instrumental in finishing this book. A special thank you to Rachel Kirsch. Editing expertise and thoughtfulness brought clarity and order to every page. Your knowledge and discipline challenged me to dig a little deeper. Thank you for helping me grow as a writer. Thank you to all the staff who proofread, typeset, designed, printed, and marketed this book. I love working with Our

Daily Bread Publishing. How blessed I am to work with a publishing house whose kingdom values I share.

Most importantly, I thank the Lord for giving us the privilege of praying for our grandchildren. In those moments when the writing was slow or finding the right illustration seemed impossible, the Lord always sent encouragement. The truth of Philippians 4:13 became a reality again. "I can do all things through Christ, who strengthens me" (WEB).

Introduction

Twenty-five years ago, our first grandchild entered the world. This sweet and lively girl introduced us to the joys of grandparenting. One by one, God sent eight more grandchildren to complete and bless our family.

Currently, this group of nine ranges in age from two to twenty-five. When they visit, we witness all the ages and stages at once. Blocks, Legos, coloring books, soccer balls, board games, video games, baking, and childhood laughter are welcome parts of our time spent together. "Grandchildren are the crown of the aged" (Proverbs 17:6).

In my twenty-five years as a grandmother, the world has changed. Our two-year-old grandson's childhood will happen in a world vastly different from that experienced by his oldest cousin.

Since the publication of *A Grandmother's Prayers* in 2015, the changes in our world have accelerated at a dizzying speed. One thing is clear to me: praying for our grandchildren is more important than ever.

Despite a shifting culture that so often confuses and concerns us, and regardless of the age differences of our grandchildren, they all have two needs that will never change. These needs exist as much in the heart of a toddler as in that of an adolescent or a young adult.

Our grandchildren need to know they are loved and valued. And they need a real and growing faith that will strengthen and help them through the hard times of life.

As grandmothers, we can play a part in fulfilling both of these needs. Our role as grandparents is subtle. Our contributions may seem small and less frequent than we would like. Yet each deposit has great potential.

The emotional and spiritual deposits we make through kind words, expressions of affection, showing an interest, sharing our own faith stories, and especially praying for the spiritual welfare of our grand-children are as precious as gold.

The world is making daily "withdrawals," draining our grandchildren's emotional and spiritual reserves. Our job is to replenish and soothe their hearts and strengthen their faith.

We can trust our heavenly Father to guard, multiply, and use each priceless deposit, no matter how small. These deposits have the power to encourage and strengthen our grandchildren in the future, regardless of the challenges they may face.

It is my hope that this devotional will help you to strategically pray for your grandchildren. Not every suggested resource will fit your need. Some topics may not apply to your situation. Others may strike a chord in your heart. If so, lean in to it and allow the Lord to lead you in focused prayer.

My prayer is that you will find within these pages something that will encourage and equip you in your role as a Christian grandmother. May the Lord guide you as you pray strategic prayers and make intentional deposits in your grandchildren's hearts.

If you are like me and sometimes wonder if prayer makes a difference, consider the words of James 5:17 regarding the power of prayer. "Elijah was a human being, even as we are. He prayed earnestly that it would not rain, and it did not rain on the land for three and a half years" (NIV).

Elijah was a human, just like us. God heard and answered his earnest prayer. He can do the same for us. May He use our prayers to raise up a generation of faithful believers to glorify Him.

day one

Keep My Babies Safe

Prayer should be the key of the day and the lock of the night.

George Herbert

In peace I will both lie down and sleep; for you alone, O LORD, make me dwell in safety.

Psalm 4:8

The small elementary school was evacuated at record pace that warm fall day. Without a hint of panic, teachers hustled hundreds of children out of the building and down the sidewalk to St. Anne's Church.

Once the children were safely inside, church staff welcomed and reassured them.

Parents had received a chilling phone message alerting them of a bomb scare. They rushed to the church, eager to hug their kids. The brief drive to reunite with their children must have felt like an eternity.

The police declared the phoned-in threat a hoax. Good news, but it did little to calm the nerves of parents and grandparents. Events like this remind us of an unfortunate truth. Our children are vulnerable. They need our protection.

Not long after, I spent the night with three grandchildren who attend that school. The youngest was missing Mom and Dad. All three (plus two dogs) crawled into the same bed and snuggled under a pink quilt. After a story or two, I prayed a bedtime prayer.

"Amen."

As I leaned over to plant a good-night kiss on each head, I saw six blue eyes staring back in disbelief. Had I forgotten something?

Nine-year-old Samantha whispered, "Grandma, Mommy always prays, 'Dear Jesus, keep my babies safe.'"

This grandma learned an unforgettable lesson that night. My daughter's tender and honest prayer for safety comforted my grandchildren. It blanketed them in peace as they drifted off. It seemed that on this night, they needed to hear those soothing words again.

What emotions do children experience when they hear loving adults pray for them by name? The very act of a loving parent praying aloud sends a much-needed message. "You are valuable. You are loved."

Hearing their own names in prayer teaches children God loves and cares for them. When parents and grandparents pray aloud for childhood needs, children absorb an important truth: Jesus cares about the smallest details of life.

I began praying for my children and grandchildren before they were born. I prayed (and still pray) for their spiritual and physical health, safety, character, and friendships.

Most of the time, I pray alone.

There is one thing I would change about my years of praying. I would have prayed aloud for them more often. How I wish each family member could have heard their names spoken hundreds of times and understood how deeply they are loved.

Maybe it is not too late.

Let us pray that . . .

- we will be faithful and constant in prayer for our grandchildren (Romans 12:12).
- we will make a daily habit of praying for our grandchildren (Mark 1:35).
- we will never give up praying for loved ones (Luke 18:1).
- we will pray in faith (1 John 5:14).
- we will share Jesus's teaching on prayer with our families (Matthew 6:9–13).

- we will find comfort in knowing Jesus intercedes for us and for our loved ones (Romans 8:34).

Heavenly Father, our hearts are comforted when others pray for us by name. The greatest comfort of all comes from knowing that Jesus prays for us. He knows our needs before we even ask. May our prayers for our children and grandchildren comfort and reassure them. Warm their hearts as we pray aloud, "Dear Jesus, keep my babies safe." Amen.

Think and Do

- Do your grandchildren know you are praying for them? They might not want our advice. But they do want our prayers.
- Do you know your grandchildren's school and extracurricular schedules? The more we know about their daily lives, the more effectively we can pray.

"Rejoice in hope, be patient in tribulation, be constant in prayer" (Romans 12:12).

"Rising very early in the morning, while it was still dark, he departed and went out to a desolate place, and there he prayed" (Mark 1:35).

"He told them a parable to the effect that they ought always to pray and not lose heart" (Luke 18:1).

"This is the confidence that we have toward him, that if we ask anything according to his will he hears us" (1 John 5:14).

"Our Father in heaven, hallowed be your name. Your kingdom come, your will be done, on earth as it is in heaven. Give us this day our daily bread, and forgive us our debts, as we also have forgiven our debtors, and lead us not into temptation, but deliver us from evil" (Matthew 6:9–13).

"Who is to condemn? Christ Jesus is the one who died—more than that, who was raised—who is at the right hand of God, who indeed is interceding for us" (Romans 8:34).

day two

Salty

Nominal Christianity is a worthless Christianity.

Dan Schillero

You are the salt of the earth, but if salt has lost its taste, how shall its saltiness be restored?

Matthew 5:13

"She was the salt of the earth."

Holding the hands of the grieving, tearful mourners shared these words as high praise for the lost loved one. They hoped to soothe the pain of grief by sharing warm memories.

The phrase "salt of the earth" requires little explanation. Even as a child I understood the meaning.

This woman lived with integrity and character. Friends and family admired her kindness, honesty, simplicity, and hard work. She and her life-giving contributions to others would be missed.

Yes, the title "salt of the earth" fit her well. She made the world a better place.

In Matthew 5:13, Jesus paid Christians the same compliment. "You are the salt of the earth." It seems that the presence of faithful Christians improves the world. Our salty influence is critical. Our saltiness can lead others to God.

Jesus's use of this word picture carried great meaning. It had deep spiritual implications.

Salt was precious in Jesus's day. Salt was the primary method of preserving food. Without salt, meat and other items quickly spoiled. Sometimes Roman soldiers received their pay in salt. Their superiors hoped their troops would prove themselves "worth their salt." Because of the supposed antibacterial qualities, rubbing salt on a newborn was common (Ezekiel 16:4). Salt had the ability to improve even tasteless food. It enhanced and highlighted flavor. Salt was considered an antidote for many poisons. If you ingested a potential poison, you would want to "take it with a grain of salt."

It is impossible to overstate the value of salt in the ancient world.

When we live for Christ as salt in the world, we restrain evil and slow the inevitable decay. We bring health and hope to the hurting. As we live with integrity and kindness, our salty testimony creates in others a thirst for the things of God.

Our saltiness provides an antidote to poisonous ideologies that threaten to accelerate the deterioration of our culture.

It is impossible to overstate the value of salty Christians in today's world.

Salty Christians make the world a better place. Salty Christians point the world to Christ.

Jesus warned of the danger of losing our saltiness. "But if the salt loses its saltiness, how can it be made salty again? It is no longer good for anything, except to be thrown out and trampled underfoot" (Matthew 5:13 NIV).

What makes us salty? How do we hold on to our influence in the world?

Pastor Dan Scherillo of Parkside Church encourages Christians to remain salty in two ways.[1]

Stay engaged. When we fearfully pull back from engaging in the world, we are losing our saltiness. We are surrendering the very influence that the world needs. The salty stay engaged. The salty understand they have a mission. In the words of Rebecca Manley Pippert's classic book, the salty get *Out of the Saltshaker and Into the World.*

Never compromise. When we cave to the culture's influence, rather than being the influencers, we lose our saltiness. Compromising biblical truth for the sake of relevance means we are dangerously close to not being "worth our salt." Salty Christians are faithful to God's Word.

Being the salt of the earth has never been more important or challenging than it is today. We are called to be salt and light wherever we are, and that begins at home. Sometimes we hesitate to be "salty" with our grandchildren. Perhaps it is fear of being seen as preachy or insensitive. Or maybe we worry that our grandchildren will think we are out of touch with culture. Whatever the reason, we can set aside our hesitation and trust that God has called us to be salt in our families and in our world. It is impossible to overstate the value of your influence.

May our saltiness rub off on our grandchildren and create a thirst that only Jesus can quench. Let us pray that someday someone will say of our grandchildren, "They are the salt of the earth." May God protect them from losing their influence as they learn to live in this world.

Let us pray that . . .

- we will understand the influence we have on our grandchildren (Matthew 5:13).
- we will be "salt" in every conversation (Colossians 4:6).
- our grandchildren's integrity will earn them the title "salt of the earth" (Proverbs 20:7).
- our grandchildren will be prepared to share their faith (1 Peter 3:15).
- our grandchildren will hold tightly to their faith and never compromise the truth (Hebrews 10:23).
- our grandchildren will engage the world and spread the gospel (Matthew 28:19–20).

Heavenly Father, we thank you for the great privilege of being "the salt of the earth." Forgive us for the times we dilute our influence through fear of engaging or by compromising the truth. We want to make the world a better place, a place where every person seeks you. We commit ourselves to engagement and faithfulness. We pray that you will help us to be salt to our families. May our words and actions

consistently reflect our love for you. Help our grandchildren grasp their mission of being "the salt of the earth." Use them to limit the decay of our culture. Light a fire within them to have a positive influence on the world. May they be known as "the salt of the earth." Amen.

Think and Do

- In 2006, Rebecca Manley Pippert's book *Out of the Saltshaker and Into the World* was named one of the top fifty books that shaped the evangelical world. In 2020, Pippert released *Stay Salt: The World Has Changed: Our Message Must Not.* Consider reading one or both of these books, and be encouraged to boldly share the changeless gospel.

- Have you been shy about engaging with your grandchildren about spiritual matters? Do you feel ill-equipped? Find a grandmother friend with whom you can pray. Together ask the Lord to give you wisdom, boldness, and gentleness to speak to your grandchildren about spiritual things. "We will tell the next generation the praiseworthy deeds of the LORD, his power, and the wonders he has done . . . so the next generation would know them, even the children yet to be born, and they in turn would tell their children" (Psalm 78: 4, 6 NIV).

"You are the salt of the earth, but if salt has lost its taste, how shall its saltiness be restored? It is no longer good for anything except to be thrown out and trampled under people's feet" (Matthew 5:13).

"Let your speech always be gracious, seasoned with salt, so that you may know how you ought to answer each person" (Colossians 4:6).

"The righteous who walks in his integrity—blessed are his children after him" (Proverbs 20:7).

"In your hearts honor Christ the Lord as holy, always being prepared to make a defense to anyone who asks you for a reason for the hope that is in you; yet do it with gentleness and respect" (1 Peter 3:15).

"Let us hold fast the confession of our hope without wavering, for he who promised is faithful" (Hebrews 10:23).

"Go therefore and make disciples of all nations, baptizing them in the name of the Father and of the Son and of the Holy Spirit, teaching them to observe all that I have commanded you. And behold, I am with you always, to the end of the age" (Matthew 28:19–20).

day three

A Birthday Prayer

There are two great days in a person's life—the day we are born and the day we discover why.

Anonymous

Gracious words are a honeycomb, sweet to the soul and healing to the bones.

Proverbs 16:24 (NIV)

No ponies. No clowns. No swim parties or sleepovers. Simply a cake with candles, Neapolitan ice cream, and a gift or two, usually a book. Birthdays were celebrated as quiet, family events.

It mattered little to my sisters and me how we marked our special day. Cake or no cake, there was one gift of which we were certain. Actually, it was the only one we cared about. We received the same gift every year and still carry it with us today. I take mine wherever I go.

Our gift was Grandma's prayer.

No birthday was complete until our grandmother recited a prayer-like poem she had learned in childhood. Before our special day, we would anticipate when and where she would offer this precious gift. Would she call and be the first in the morning to wish a happy birthday? Perhaps we could walk to her house and wait patiently on the porch swing for her to open the screen door and invite us into her yellow kitchen. Maybe she would recite it at the end of the day as we shared our ice cream.

Many happy returns of the day of thy birth,
May sunshine and gladness be given.
May God in His mercy prepare you on earth
For a beautiful birthday in heaven.
(Alice Jacobs and Ermina C. Lincoln)

With four short lines, Grandma invited God into the celebration. Once she spoke those words, the entire day felt like a party. Clearly, Grandma longed for each of her granddaughters to enjoy beautiful lives with faith in God.

Today my sisters and I often compete for who will be the first to say Grandma's prayer on another sister's birthday. When it is my turn to receive the cherished blessing, the same image flashes through my mind as when Grandma said these words to me as a seven-year-old. I see a carefree little girl skipping on a sunlit path, holding Someone's hand.

Grandma's prayer taught me I was loved and never alone.

The birthday prayer has carried me from year to year. I credit some of my optimism to this yearly tradition. Grandma's consistent, loving words offered hope. We could have received no more precious a gift than the gift of her prayer.

I am certain my quiet grandmother had no idea of the power of her words or the importance of this small tradition. I wonder if she knew how eagerly we wanted to hear her speak those loving words.

Like my grandmother, we are often unaware of the power of our words. We are blind to the importance of the small family traditions that keep us connected and hopeful.

Our grandchildren need hopeful, encouraging, inspiring words from the people they love. I pray the Lord will give us the eyes to see the significance of even the smallest word of encouragement. May we renew our efforts to share simple, special moments with our grandchildren and reassure them that they are loved and never alone.

Let us pray that . . .

- we will grasp the importance of the words we speak to family (Proverbs 25:11).
- we will guard our speech from negativity (Psalm 141:3).

23

- we will make the most of our time with our grandchildren without being preachy (Colossians 4:6; 1 Peter 3:15).
- our grandchildren will experience the hope that God has promised (Romans 15:13).
- our grandchildren will believe God knew them even before they were born and affirm the sanctity of life for all (Psalm 139:13–18).

Heavenly Father, thank you for the kind words spoken to us by the people we loved. We treasure those memories. Give us wisdom as we choose words to bless our families. Help us to remember that above all else, our grandchildren need the hope that only Jesus gives. May we make the most of the special, little moments. May our words give the gift of hope to the hearts of our grandchildren. Amen.

Think and Do

- A friend made this suggestion for structuring our prayer times: Each month, use your grandchild's day of birth as a way of scheduling prayer focused on that specific child. Let your child know that each month you will be praying on that day.
- *The Gift That I Can Give* by Kathie Lee Gifford teaches children that gifts don't have to be large or expensive. Sometimes the best gifts are words of encouragement.
- Do you recall any special family traditions shared in your childhood home? Did they provide a sense of security? Are there family traditions you share with your grandchildren?

"A word fitly spoken is like apples of gold in a setting of silver" (Proverbs 25:11).

"Set a guard, O LORD, over my mouth; keep watch over the door of my lips" (Psalm 141:3).

"Let your speech always be gracious, seasoned with salt, so that you may know how you ought to answer each person" (Colossians 4:6).

"In your hearts honor Christ the Lord as holy, always being prepared to make a defense to anyone who asks you for a reason for the hope that is in you; yet do it with gentleness and respect" (1 Peter 3:15).

"May the God of hope fill you with all joy and peace in believing, so that by the power of the Holy Spirit you may abound in hope" (Romans 15:13).

"My frame was not hidden from you, when I was being made in secret, intricately woven in the depths of the earth. Your eyes saw my unformed substance; in your book were written, every one of them, the days that were formed for me, when as yet there was none of them" (Psalm 139:15–16).

day four

Deliverer

Deliver us from every evil thing that may entangle our affections and harden our hearts.

William Tiptaft

Lead us not into temptation, but deliver us from the evil one.

Matthew 6:13 (NIV)

Baby locks on cabinets. Covers for electrical plugs. Sharp objects all hidden. Medications under lock and key. It is time to babyproof Grandma's house again.

With each new addition to the family, I am reminded of the vulnerability of children. The drive to explore has led many a curious toddler to danger. Objects that pose no threat to adults can be lethal for a child.

Protecting children is a full-time job for parents, grandparents, teachers, daycare workers, or anyone who cares for the welfare of children. Guarding the physical safety of children is critical. Watching over the moral and spiritual safety of little ones is equally if not more essential to their ultimate well-being.

The Lord gave His disciples a template for prayer in Matthew 6:7–13. The final line in the Lord's Prayer seems especially relevant in our current situation. As the world grows increasingly dark, we pray the words of Jesus on behalf of ourselves and our children. "Lead us not into temptation, but deliver us from the evil one" (v. 13 NIV).

While the meaning of this verse is not entirely clear to me, it is crystal clear that Jesus acknowledged the reality of temptation and evil in our world. Our prayer is for protection and help against the attacks of the enemy.

On His final night with His disciples, Jesus prayed a similar prayer on behalf of His friends. "My prayer is not that you take them out of the world but that you protect them from the evil one" (John 17:15 NIV).

Many grandparents are concerned (even distressed) over the evil their grandchildren face. We are no longer in denial that dangers exist.

After years of devoting ourselves to their physical safety, we feel increasingly powerless to protect them from harm. But that isn't true. We are not helpless.

We simply need to do what Jesus did for His disciples. We need to follow His loving and powerful example.

We need to pray.

We can ask the Father to protect our loved ones from the assaults of the evil one. We need to look to Jesus as our one and only deliverer. We must hang on to the belief that Jesus will make a way of escape from temptation.

Of all the prayers we could lift to heaven, perhaps this is the most important: "Lord, we place our children and grandchildren into your hands. We ask you to protect them from the temptations and attacks of the evil one."

Let us pray that . . .

- our grandchildren will submit themselves to God and the enemy will flee (James 4:7).
- our grandchildren's faith will be nurtured (Ephesians 6:4).
- our grandchildren will walk in the Spirit, not in the flesh (Galatians 5:16).
- our grandchildren will be strong in the Lord and clothe themselves in the armor of God (Ephesians 6:10–17).
- our grandchildren will be protected from the evil one (John 17:15–16).

- our grandchildren will be sanctified by the word of God (John 17:17).
- our grandchildren will turn to Jesus for a way of escape (1 Corinthians 10:13).
- our grandchildren will acknowledge Jesus as their deliverer (Psalm 18:2).

Heavenly Father, our comfort is in knowing that Jesus is our deliverer. Give each member of our family the inner strength needed to reject the enemy's tactics. In your mercy, deliver our loved ones from the deceptions of the adversary. When temptations overwhelm, may Jesus make a way of escape. We pray as Jesus prayed. Deliver our loved ones from the evil one. Amen.

Think and Do

- Do you want to offer your grandkids some tools for navigating the world? The armor of God is a good place to start. Tony Evans's children's book *A Kid's Guide to the Armor of God* contains helpful insights for eight- to twelve-year-olds.
- First Corinthians 10:13 tells us that God provides a way of escape during temptation. Do you know any "escape" stories that would help a grandchild understand this truth?

"Submit yourselves therefore to God. Resist the devil, and he will flee from you" (James 4:7).

"Fathers, do not provoke your children to anger, but bring them up in the discipline and instruction of the Lord" (Ephesians 6:4).

"Walk by the Spirit, and you will not gratify the desires of the flesh" (Galatians 5:16).

"Be strong in the Lord and in the strength of his might. Put on the whole armor of God, that you may be able to stand against the schemes of the devil" (Ephesians 6:10–11).

"I do not ask that you take them out of the world, but that you keep them from the evil one. They are not of the world, just as I am not of the world" (John 17:15–16).

"Sanctify them in the truth; your word is truth" (John 17:17).

"No temptation has overtaken you that is not common to man. God is faithful, and he will not let you be tempted beyond your ability, but with the temptation he will also provide the way of escape, that you may be able to endure it" (1 Corinthians 10:13).

"The Lord is my rock and my fortress and my deliverer, my God, my rock, in whom I take refuge, my shield, and the horn of my salvation, my stronghold" (Psalm 18:2).

day five

The Catcher

Preach often to troubled hearts.
Anonymous

Cast all your anxiety on him because he cares for you.
1 Peter 5:7 (NIV)

"It's a hit!" Still clutching the bat, five-year-old Noah headed toward the pink jump rope that served as a makeshift first base. Realizing no one was in pursuit, he ran past second (an orange jump rope) and began to zigzag, ending up on the far end of the neighbor's yard.

"Noah! Come back!"

Clearly, we have a lot of work to do with the Swatkowski baseball team. Now that we have five little grandsons close in age, we also could use some real equipment.

Eight-year-old Aiden has a good handle on the world of baseball.

"I'll be the catcher, Grandma." Crouching behind home plate (yes, another jump rope), he adopted the snarling demeanor of a professional. With Aiden behind the plate, I had one job. Get the ball past his nine-year-old cousin and into the hands of our brown-eyed catcher in the making.

Watching my grandsons play ball gives me a visual for what 1 Peter 5:7 commands us to do. We are to cast all our worries on Jesus, because He cares for us.

Cast means "to throw upon and thus to deposit with."[2] The verb tense used here indicates a once-and-for-all action. It is not a wild casting of our anxiety. It is not throwing it away only to pick it back up again. It is the kind of casting that has a specific and permanent destination.

In baseball, the pitcher is often the star of the show. But it's the catcher who is vital to the pitcher's success. Every play requires his keen skills. Hand in glove, at the ready, eyes locked with the pitcher, the catcher is perfectly poised. He doesn't twitch a muscle while his teammate winds up and hurls the ball. Our catcher friend is not satisfied that he has done his job until he hears that unmistakable slap of leather against leather.

Nothing gets past him.

What worries or weighty concerns for your grandchildren are you holding on to today? Do you know you can throw those worries straight into the waiting hands of Jesus?

He is poised and ready. He has His eyes on you. He is waiting for you to let go and throw all those cares into His loving hands.

He will not miss. You can count on Him.

Let us make a commitment once and for all. When the load gets too heavy to carry, when anxiety threatens to overwhelm us, we will cast all our cares into the waiting hands of Jesus.

Let us encourage our grandchildren to cast all their cares on Jesus as well. It is time to assume the wind-up position.

Let us pray that . . .

- we will model prayer over anxiety and trust over worry (Philippians 4:6–7).
- our grandchildren will trust Jesus in the troubles of life (John 16:33).
- our grandchildren will trust God to supply their needs (Philippians 4:19).
- our grandchildren will know God is aware of the tiniest details of their lives (Matthew 10:29–31).

- our grandchildren will know that God is their helper (Hebrews 13:6).
- our grandchildren will cast all their cares upon the Lord (1 Peter 5:7).

Heavenly Father, we see the struggles and challenges our grandchildren face. It causes us great worry. You invite us to throw all our cares on you. Because your love for our grandchildren far exceeds our own, we choose to cast all our cares in your direction. Help us to leave our cares with you. May we have such a calmness of spirit that our grandchildren will ask how they too can have peace with God. Use us to encourage our grandchildren to pitch all their cares to you. Amen.

Think and Do

- Children are like sponges. They absorb the anxiety around them. Maybe the reverse is true as well. They can absorb the peace in your home. How can you communicate peace to your grandchildren?
- An inning or two of baseball might provide an opportunity for a quick and informal object lesson.
- As a young believer, I was encouraged by older believers to "leave my cares at the altar." I found great freedom in leaving my cares with God. I currently have a prayer bowl, where I leave slips of paper with written prayers. This bowl symbolizes my desire to leave my troubles with God.

"Do not be anxious about anything, but in everything by prayer and supplication with thanksgiving let your requests be made known to God. And the peace of God, which surpasses all understanding, will guard your hearts and your minds in Christ Jesus" (Philippians 4:6–7).

"I have said these things to you, that in me you may have peace. In the world you will have tribulation. But take heart; I have overcome the world" (John 16:33).

"My God will supply every need of yours according to his riches in glory in Christ Jesus" (Philippians 4:19).

"Are not two sparrows sold for a penny? And not one of them will fall to the ground apart from your Father. But even the hairs of your head are all numbered. Fear not, therefore; you are of more value than many sparrows" (Matthew 10:29–31).

"So we can confidently say, 'The Lord is my helper; I will not fear; what can man do to me?'" (Hebrews 13:6).

"Humble yourselves, therefore, under God's mighty hand, that he may lift you up in due time. Cast all your anxiety on him because he cares for you" (1 Peter 5:6–7 NIV).

day six

Get Wisdom

As we trust God to give us wisdom for today's decisions, He will lead us a step at a time into what He wants us to be doing in the future.

Theodore Epp

The beginning of wisdom is this: Get wisdom. Though it cost you all you have, get understanding.

Proverbs 4:7 (NIV)

A Mustang? A truck—a *big* one?

Kevin was in the market for a car. After months of saving and weeks of searching, he found a clean, used car that had only been driven by an eighty-year-old widow. His common sense and need for dependability overshadowed his dream of a sleek, powerful, fast car.

A wise decision made by a mature and wise twenty-one-year-old.

We are living in an unwise world. Our grandchildren are confronted with advice from an unwise environment. For some, decisions are made on the basis of emotions or novel philosophies that have no enduring foundation.

Tossed and pummeled by the waves of their own emotions, young people struggle to find purpose. No wonder anxiety and depression plague this age group. Suicide hotlines report frighteningly high numbers of calls from young adults.

Our young people need help.

What our young people need most is wisdom.

Years ago, I gleaned a simple truth from a book by Andy Stanley, *The Best Question Ever.*[3] From this insightful book, I learned to ask myself the question, "What is the wisest thing I can do in this situation?"

A switch flipped in my brain! After years of fellowship with other Christians, Bible studies, prayer, access to spiritual counsel, and life experiences, we have access to wisdom. In nearly every dilemma, we can discern (based upon the truth we've been given) the wisest thing to do.

The simple question clears away the emotional fog that routinely clouds our view. In asking the question, we elevate the role of biblical wisdom in decision-making.

Asking the question draws something out of us that feels right.

On more than one occasion, I've asked a young person this question, "What is the wisest thing you could do in this situation?" Each time, he had a calm, quiet, mature answer based on scriptural principles. We need to give young people the opportunity to tap into the wisdom of Scripture that is already stored up in their hearts.

"If any of you lacks wisdom," James 1:5 says, "you should ask God, who gives generously" (NIV).

Indeed, God generously gives wisdom. He has filled up a storehouse of wisdom in His Word. He provides the counsel of godly people. To all, He offers the gift of common sense. As believers, we are blessed with the Holy Spirit to guide us.

God generously gives wisdom.

Wisdom is accessible. We just have to look in the right places. We have to ask ourselves the right questions. We need to spend time with the right people. We need to be willing to pay the price for wisdom.

Wisdom often comes to us in snippets of understanding. But if we seek, it does come. It helps us move toward the right path one step at a time. "And he will make your paths straight" (Proverbs 3:6 NIV).

I long for my grandchildren to have a storehouse of wisdom to draw on throughout life. What is the wisest thing I can do to encourage them to seek biblical wisdom?

I can pray. I can pray they will have the fear of the Lord that is the beginning of wisdom (Psalm 111:10). I can pray they will follow the advice of Solomon to his son: "Get wisdom" at any cost (Proverbs 4:7).

Let us pray that . . .

- our grandchildren will fear the Lord and gain understanding and wisdom (Proverbs 9:10).
- our grandchildren will humbly accept the wisdom of others (1 Peter 5:5).
- our grandchildren will listen to wise advice (Proverbs 12:15).
- our grandchildren will live and walk as the wise (Ephesians 5:15–16).
- our grandchildren will turn to God for wisdom (James 1:5).
- our grandchildren will make the search for wisdom a lifelong pursuit (Proverbs 4:7).

Heavenly Father, we confess that we have not always lived wisely. We choose to pursue wisdom. Thank you for generously giving us access to the wisdom of your Word, the counsel of wise believers, and the gentle voice of the Holy Spirit. We pray for our grandchildren struggling to make sense of this unwise world. Reveal to them the difference your wisdom can make in a life. May they have the fear of the Lord and a knowledge of the Holy One. May the pursuit of biblical wisdom become a defining trait of our grandchildren's generation. Amen.

Think and Do

- Classic children's literature is filled with examples of wise and unwise people. *Heidi*, by Johanna Spyri, offers many such examples. Use read-aloud time to help your grandchildren see wisdom at work in the characters of their favorite books.
- Are you facing a difficult life decision right now? Where will you turn for help in making that decision? What is the wisest thing you can do today?

- You may find *The Best Question Ever* by Andy Stanley helpful and encouraging.
- A Proverb a day can provide wisdom for daily life.

"The fear of the LORD is the beginning of wisdom, and the knowledge of the Holy One is insight" (Proverbs 9:10).

"You who are younger, be subject to the elders. Clothe yourselves, all of you, with humility toward one another, for 'God opposes the proud but gives grace to the humble'" (1 Peter 5:5).

"The way of a fool is right in his own eyes, but a wise man listens to advice" (Proverbs 12:15).

"Look carefully then how you walk, not as unwise but as wise, making the best use of the time, because the days are evil" (Ephesians 5:15–16).

"If any of you lacks wisdom, let him ask God, who gives generously to all without reproach, and it will be given him" (James 1:5).

"The beginning of wisdom is this: Get wisdom. Though it cost all you have, get understanding" (Proverbs 4:7 NIV).

day seven

The Repair Shop

What a wonderful thing it is to be able to contribute to the restoration of someone's health.

Dr. Ben Carson

After you have suffered a little while, the God of all grace, who has called you to his eternal glory in Christ, will himself restore, confirm, strengthen, and establish you.

1 Peter 5:10

Placing the scuffed gold watch on the workbench, the gentleman began to share his family's story. The once elegant piece had belonged to his grandmother. In the 1940s she had sewn the watch into the seam of her dress. It remained hidden there the entire four years she was imprisoned in Auschwitz. It would mean so much to the family for the item to be repaired.

The silver-haired woman whispered her story as the repairman reverently held the battered violin. With make-do patches here and there, every inch, every scratch, every worn spot told the story of a captive Jewish grandfather who bequeathed to his family a love of music. Tearfully, she expressed the hope that she would one day hear again the sweet notes of the treasured instrument.

A one-hundred-year-old butter churn, long forgotten by everyone but a loving granddaughter, was an emotional reminder of a simpler time. Could the Repair Shop restore the prized churn that represented the family legacy of hard work and love? The granddaughter's one desire was to honor the grandmother she adored.

These are just a few of the stories from BBC's series, *The Repair Shop*.[4] The objects presented to the restorers at the Repair Shop are priceless; the family stories moving and inspirational.

Yet it is the mindset of the restorers that has grabbed my heart.

Each project is approached with reverence and respect. Making a family treasure like new is not the goal. Restoring it in accordance with the owner's wishes is the priority.

The repair is neither forced nor hurried. Hours of research precede the actual work. Materials are chosen carefully to match the original makeup of the item. With great expertise and true humility, the craftsmen work to honor the history of the prized heirloom.

Often the restorer intentionally leaves some of the scratches, dents, or signs of wear and tear.

After all, aren't our scars part of our stories?

We live in a hurting world filled with heartbroken people in need of repair. Some of the brokenhearted are our children, grandchildren, siblings, spouses, or even parents. How we approach our small part in their restoration and healing is important.

Humility, respect, gentleness, and time are key to initiating authentic restoration.

In Matthew 12:19–20, Jesus quotes a passage from Isaiah that describes the demeanor and character of the coming Messiah. "He will not quarrel or cry out; no one will hear his voice in the streets. A bruised reed he will not break, and a smoldering wick he will not snuff out" (NIV). Jesus did not come to snap and dispose of bruised reeds. He did not come to extinguish the last flicker of a smoldering light.

He came to restore and repair.

While others might see bruised and broken people as expendable or an annoyance, Jesus came with humility to care for those damaged by life or marred by their own sin.

He saw their scars as part of their story. He dealt gently with the bruised and broken. Their scars in no way diminished their value.

May the Lord help us listen to and honor the concerns of others, even those in our own families. May our demeanor be that of humility, gentleness, and respect. And may our grandchildren grow into the compassionate, respectful people we know they can be.

Let us pray that . . .

- we will help to bear the burdens of the hurting (Galatians 6:2).
- we will weep with those who weep, especially with family members, friends, and fellow believers (Romans 12:15).
- our grandchildren will experience the nearness of God when their hearts are heavy (Psalm 34:18; 56:8).
- our grandchildren will turn to God for healing of their broken hearts (Psalm 147:3).
- our grandchildren will have godly friends who will lovingly restore them (Galatians 6:1).
- our grandchildren will grow into humble and compassionate people (Galatians 6:9–10).

Heavenly Father, we thank you for dealing so tenderly with the broken and bruised. We pray for our family members who are broken, battered, and scarred. Grant us the humility to be sincere listeners willing to comfort, care, and wipe away their tears. Give us patience. Guard our lips from harsh words that will cause more pain. May our homes and churches become places of restoration and repair. Amen.

Think and Do

- Read Galatians 6:1. What instructions does the writer give to us when we are restoring someone who has fallen? What principles apply equally well to those who have been injured by life's tragedies? Note that the ultimate goal is restoring someone to usefulness for the kingdom.
- *The Repair Shop* can be seen on BBC. Every episode is heartwarming.

"Bear one another's burdens, and so fulfill the law of Christ" (Galatians 6:2).

"Rejoice with those who rejoice, weep with those who weep" (Romans 12:15).

"The LORD is near to the brokenhearted and saves the crushed in spirit" (Psalm 34:18).

"You have kept count of my tossings; put my tears in your bottle. Are they not in your book?" (Psalm 56:8).

"He heals the brokenhearted and binds up their wounds" (Psalm 147:3).

"Brothers and sisters, if someone is caught in a sin, you who live by the Spirit should restore that person gently. But watch yourselves, or you also may be tempted" (Galatians 6:1 NIV).

"Let us not grow weary of doing good, for in due season we will reap, if we do not give up. So then, as we have opportunity, let us do good to everyone, and especially to those who are of the household of faith" (Galatians 6:9–10).

day eight

The Bonus Family

None knows the weight of another's burden.

George Herbert

A stepparent is so much more than just a parent: they made the choice to love when they didn't have to.

Anonymous

Do not neglect to do good and to share what you have, for such sacrifices are pleasing to God.

Hebrews 13:16

It is true. In spite of negative perceptions, millions of children benefit from the love of a stepparent.

Thomas Lincoln moved his family from the woods of Kentucky to Pigeon Fork, Indiana. His hopes of providing a better future for his family crumbled when his wife, Nancy, died of milk sickness.

Overcome with grief, Thomas struggled to provide care for young Abe and his sister, Sarah. Thomas made a visit to his hometown in Kentucky. He called upon a family friend, the widowed Sarah Bush, and promptly proposed.

Sarah had three children of her own.

She quickly set things right in the Lincoln household. She made a stable, clean home for Thomas and the children. She also saw Abe's potential. In spite of her own lack of education, she devoted herself to acquiring books for the young boy.

Historians suggest that it was Sarah Lincoln's unshakable faith in Abe's abilities and character that shaped him for his future role as president. Abe called her his "best friend in this world."[5]

She was a stepmom.

Combining families due to divorce or the untimely death of a parent is not new. For centuries, premature death made this dynamic critical to family survival.

What is new is the term *bonus family*.

A bonus is something given as a reward. It is unexpected. After the pain of divorce or loss, welcoming bonus grandchildren can be a joy and an unanticipated blessing from God.

Grandparents who consider the addition of grandchildren through remarriage as a bonus often find the experience less stressful. In spite of the obvious challenges, they say yes to the opportunity to love and nurture a child.

When we welcome a child, we are engaged in kingdom work and honor the Lord. "Whoever receives this child in my name receives me, and whoever receives me receives him who sent me. For he who is least among you all is the one who is great" (Luke 9:48).

Are you a bonus grandparent? If you are, God bless you. Your love and acceptance are bonuses in the life of a child. God knows why He chose to bring this child into your family. You can trust in His wisdom.

God works all things for good, even from difficult situations. Perhaps bonus grandparents can play a small role in the healing and redemption of a family.

Let us pray for bonus family members and offer them our love and support. Let us pray for those bonus grandchildren who are still in the process of adjusting. May the Lord grant them strength and wisdom as they grow together.

Let us pray that . . .

- bonus grandchildren will feel welcomed (Mark 10:13–16).
- bonus grandchildren will be received as gifts from the Lord (Psalm 127:3).

- bonus family members will grow in tenderhearted kindness toward one another (Ephesians 4:32).
- bonus grandparents will honor boundaries and respect parental decisions (Philippians 2:4).
- bonus grandparents will boldly pray for their families in times of need (Hebrews 4:16).
- bonus grandchildren will feel loved and be nurtured in the faith (John 21:15).

Heavenly Father, we pray for those families in the process of blending. We admire their courage and determination. Fill them with love for one another. Surround them with friends and family who will provide support and care. We pray that the children welcomed into these homes will feel loved and accepted by stepparents and step-grandparents. Create a new family that brings honor and glory to your name. May these homes be places where children flourish and grow. Amen.

Think and Do

- Do you have bonus grandchildren? What challenges do you face? Where can you find emotional and prayer support?
- *Building Love Together in Blended Families: The 5 Love Languages and Becoming Stepfamily Smart* by Gary Chapman and Ron Deal has been helpful to many families on this journey.

"They were bringing children to him that he might touch them, and the disciples rebuked them. But when Jesus saw it, he was indignant and said to them, 'Let the children come to me; do not hinder them, for to such belongs the kingdom of God'" (Mark 10:13–14).

"Behold, children are a heritage from the LORD, the fruit of the womb a reward" (Psalm 127:3).

"Be kind to one another, tenderhearted, forgiving one another, as God in Christ forgave you" (Ephesians 4:32).

"Let each of you look not only to his own interests, but also to the interests of others" (Philippians 2:4).

"Let us then with confidence draw near to the throne of grace, that we may receive mercy and find grace to help in time of need" (Hebrews 4:16).

"When they had finished breakfast, Jesus said to Simon Peter, 'Simon, son of John, do you love me more than these?' He said to him, 'Yes, Lord; you know that I love you.' He said to him, 'Feed my lambs'" (John 21:15).

day nine

Honor

If you build a society in which children honor their parents, your society will long survive.

Dennis Prager

Stand up in the presence of the aged, show respect for the elderly and revere your God. I am the LORD.

Leviticus 19:32 (NIV)

C. S. Lewis once wrote, "Autumn is really the best of the seasons: and I'm not sure that old age isn't the best part of life."[6] For some, these words ring true. For many, declining health and loneliness make maintaining this perspective an honest challenge.

In the final months of her life, my mother-in-law grew increasingly frail. Spending her days in her red recliner, we watched as she became weaker and quieter. She often whispered, "Why is God leaving me here?" In the autumn of her life, she might not have agreed with the words of Mr. Lewis.

Laverne feared she had little left to give to the people she loved. We did not agree.

As we shared one last meal with her at her youngest son's home, it was clear God still had a purpose for this ninety-four-year-old.

While everyone ate their burgers and chips, Laverne closed her eyes and began to pray in a stronger voice than we had heard in months. Moments before, she struggled with names. Now, on that beautiful summer evening, she not only remembered names, but recalled circumstances. She poured out her heart to God on behalf of her family.

She was still with us because we needed her. We needed her sincere and heartfelt prayers.

Another ninety-four-year-old, my friend Phyllis, offered an inspiring reason for longevity. The recent death of an older Christian provoked an honest discussion among Phyllis and her same-aged friends.

Once again the question was asked, "Why is God leaving us here?"

Phyllis wisely responded, "Because young people need someone to honor." How true.

The benefits of honoring the elderly accrue not only to the honoree but also to the one doing the honoring. Honoring the elderly enriches everyone and causes even children to flourish.

Honoring the elderly develops character. Considering another person's needs above one's own fosters humility and generosity. Visiting and offering help to someone who cannot return the favor is an act of selflessness. Acknowledging the worth of even the frailest among us shows mercy.

Each gesture of respect transforms both the one being honored and the one doing the honoring. The honoring of the generations that have gone before creates a more stable society.

The fifth commandment is the only one with a promise attached: "Honor your father and your mother, so that you may live long in the land the LORD your God is giving you" (Exodus 20:12 NIV).

Paul expands on the value of honoring parents in Ephesians 6:1–3. "Children, obey your parents in the Lord, for this is right. 'Honor your father and mother' (this is the first commandment with a promise), 'that it may go well with you and that you may live long in the land.'"

Grandparents hope and pray that everything will go well in the lives of their grandchildren. According to Scripture, a satisfying and productive life is a positive and natural outcome of respecting one's elders.

The mercy, generosity, selflessness, humility, kindness, and self-respect fostered by respecting the elderly can steer a young person's life in a positive direction.

Young people need someone to honor.

May the Lord grant us peace as we trust Him in the autumn season. May we continue to grow in our faith and become grandparents worthy of honor and respect. May our grandchildren be known for the selfless ways they honor and respect the elderly.

Let us pray that . . .

- we will not demand respect, but rather become worthy of honor (Titus 2:2–3).
- we will recognize God's sovereignty over the length and purpose of our lives (Psalms 139:16; 92:14).
- our grandchildren will show honor to those older than themselves (Leviticus 19:32).
- our grandchildren will honor and obey their parents and please the Lord (Ephesians 6:2).
- our grandchildren will experience the blessings that come with showing respect (Exodus 20:12).
- our grandchildren will lead the way in showing respect to whom it is due (Romans 13:7).

Heavenly Father, help us to follow the faithful examples of those who have gone before us. May we become people worthy of honor and respect. In the autumn of life, keep us from complaining and bitterness. Protect our grandchildren from the secular philosophies that gauge human worth by appearance and productivity. Help them to honor and serve their elders with sincerity. It is our hearts' desire that things would go well for our grandchildren. May their selflessness and care for others lead them to a beautiful, satisfying, reverent life. Amen.

Think and Do

- Years ago, I heard of a Larry King interview with Billy Graham. Mr. King wondered if the evangelist found turning seventy-five difficult. As closely as I remember, this was Dr. Graham's reply:

"I guess I am the age God wants me to be." Are you content with your age? Read Philippians 4:12 (NIV).

- Have you prayed for a long life? Now that God has granted your request, what will you do with it?

"Older women likewise are to be reverent in behavior" (Titus 2:3).

"Your eyes saw my unformed substance; in your book were written, every one of them, the days that were formed for me, when as yet there was none of them" (Psalm 139:16).

"They still bear fruit in old age; they are ever full of sap and green" (Psalm 92:14).

"You shall stand up before the gray head and honor the face of an old man, and you shall fear your God: I am the LORD" (Leviticus 19:32).

"'Honor your father and mother' (this is the first commandment with a promise), 'that it may go well with you and that you may live long in the land'" (Ephesians 6:2–3).

"Honor your father and your mother, that your days may be long in the land that the LORD your God is giving you" (Exodus 20:12).

"Pay to all what is owed to them: taxes to whom taxes are owed, revenue to whom revenue is owed, respect to whom respect is owed, honor to whom honor is owed" (Romans 13:7).

day ten

One Drop of Mercy

When God intends great mercy for his people, the first thing he does is to set them praying.

Matthew Henry

Let us then with confidence draw near to the throne of grace, that we may receive mercy and find grace to help in time of need.

Hebrews 4:16

The sidewalk in front of our daughter's house is an art gallery. With chunks of chalk strewn everywhere, our grandkids spend hours drawing flowers, smiley faces, puppy dogs, and portraits of their friends.

In the spring of 2020, ten-year-old Madelyn carefully drew a schoolhouse. This girl loves school and learning. Above her masterpiece she wrote words that touched my heart. "I want to be in school."

Madelyn's angst was felt by us all. Mental health experts wonder what long-term effects the lost year will have on the nation's children.

Children were not alone in the feelings of isolation. We all wanted to be at school or work. We wanted to visit family and friends, attend birthday parties, and celebrate weddings. We wanted to take a vacation. We wanted to go to church.

We wanted our lives back.

Resilient parents (some who thought they would be shopping for graduation supplies) were shopping for masks. Hand sanitizer replaced sunscreen. Store employees pointed digital thermometers at complete strangers. Brave healthcare workers struggled under the weight of pounds of protective gear.

The quarantine was just the beginning of our problems. City after city endured days of unrest and fear.

The stress of 2020 won't soon be forgotten.

Every day was a fresh reminder of our own limitations. Sadness hovered over our house like a cloud.

Until one Sunday morning. During a streaming church service, we heard a Christian leader include a hopeful phrase in his morning prayer. "Lord, we know that you could eradicate this virus with just one drop of your mercy."

I nearly jumped out of my chair with joy.

One drop of God's mercy. Just one. There is comfort in the thought of God's boundless mercy. God's mercy is always the answer to our heartaches and fears.

"The steadfast love of the LORD never ceases; his mercies never come to an end; they are new every morning; great is your faithfulness" (Lamentations 3:22–23).

Matthew Henry's words encourage me. "When God intends great mercy for his people the first thing he does is to set them praying."[7] Right now in hundreds of cities and churches, God has set people to praying. These believers are obeying God's ongoing call for repentance and intercessory prayer.

They are asking God to pour out His mercy on us all.

Scripture teaches that God's mercy and healing are poured out in response to our confession and repentance. "If my people who are called by my name humble themselves, and pray and seek my face and turn from their wicked ways, then I will hear from heaven and will forgive their sin and heal their land" (2 Chronicles 7:14).

Repentance isn't easy. But it is the surest path to mercy.

Confessing our national sins is one thing—we can easily distance ourselves from responsibility. Confessing our own sinfulness is a more painful matter. Yet if we confess with sincerity and humility, God promises to pour out His mercy and heal us.

In His mercy, He can even help little kids return to the schools and friendships they love.

We need God's mercy as much today as we did in 2020. The good news is God's mercy never runs out. It is inexhaustible. It is new every morning.

God will shower us with His mercy when we humbly repent. We can count on it.

We can also trust that in response to our repentance, God will send times of refreshing for our souls. "Repent therefore, and turn back, that your sins may be blotted out, that times of refreshing may come from the presence of the Lord, and that he may send the Christ appointed for you, Jesus" (Acts 3:19–20).

As a grandparent, I want my grandchildren to experience the mercy of God. I want their souls to be refreshed and thrilled by His mercy and grace. I pray God will pour out His mercy on us all.

Let us pray that . . .

- all people, everywhere, including those in our home, would repent (Acts 17:30).
- our children and grandchildren would not hide their sins (Proverbs 28:13).
- our grandchildren would have the godly sorrow that leads to salvation (2 Corinthians 7:10).
- our grandchildren will call on God for mercy (Psalm 30:8).
- our grandchildren would proclaim repentance and salvation to everyone (Luke 24:47).
- our grandchildren will experience times of refreshing from the Lord (Acts 3:19–20).

Heavenly Father, we have never been more desperate for your mercy than now. Thank you for using these difficult days to draw us to a deeper dependence upon you. Search our hearts and show us any wicked way in us. We confess our sins to you. We accept the forgiveness you so freely offer. We ask you to pour out your mercy on our

families, friends, churches, communities. Send times of refreshing to our aching, weary hearts. Send sweet times of refreshing especially to our children and grandchildren. Amen.

Think and Do

- Do you have a regular practice of confession? Take time to search your heart and ask God to point out which of these sins is hindering your relationship with Him: addiction, anger, apathy, bearing grudges, bitterness, blaming, complaining, controlling, coveting, critical spirit, deceit, disobedience, divisiveness, envy, failing to do good, failing to honor parents, favoritism, gossip, greed, hatred, idle words, idolatry, insensitivity to others, irresponsibility, keeping things that don't belong to you, judging, laziness, lust, lying, malice, materialism, neglecting God's Word, neglecting the poor and needy, neglecting prayer, obsession with entertainment, obstinance, pride, quarreling, racism, rebellion, resentment, selfishness, sexual sin, slander, stealing, troublemaking, unfaithfulness, worry.

- Meditate on Hebrews 7:25 and the great mercy of God: "Therefore he is able to save completely those who come to God through him, because he always lives to intercede for them" (NIV).

- Do you want to introduce a grandchild to the concept of confession? *Arlo and the Great Big Cover-Up* by Betsy Childs Howard is just right for children ages three to seven.

"The times of ignorance God overlooked, but now he commands all people everywhere to repent" (Acts 17:30).

"Whoever conceals his transgressions will not prosper, but he who confesses and forsakes them will obtain mercy" (Proverbs 28:13).

"Godly grief produces a repentance that leads to salvation without regret, whereas worldly grief produces death" (2 Corinthians 7:10).

"To you, O Lord, I cry, and to the Lord I plead for mercy" (Psalm 30:8).

"Thus it is written, that the Christ should suffer and on the third day rise from the dead, and that repentance for the forgiveness of sins should be proclaimed in his name to all nations, beginning from Jerusalem" (Luke 24:46–47).

"Repent therefore, and turn back, that your sins may be blotted out, that times of refreshing may come from the presence of the Lord, and that he may send the Christ appointed for you, Jesus" (Acts 3:19–20).

day eleven

Count Your Joys

Thou that hast giv'n so much to me, give one thing more, a grateful heart.

George Herbert

Giving thanks always and for everything to God the Father in the name of our Lord Jesus Christ.

Ephesians 5:20

"I'm so stressed." This complaint from seven-year-old Holden surprised me.

"What are you stressed about, buddy?"

He grew breathless as his words tumbled out. "Sometimes I just start thinking about stuff and my head starts spinning and I get so stressed."

Rolling her eyes, his nine-year-old sister remarked, "He says that all the time."

Fortunately, the eleven-year-old (a born problem solver) offered a remedy. "I read if you think of three things you are thankful for every day, in twenty-one days you will be a happier person. Is that true, Grandma?"

"I think it is. Let's try."

The girls quickly listed all the things for which they were grateful. Holden was the last to share his list and was determined to outdo his sisters. When he reached number thirteen, his sisters asked, "Are you feeling better?"

"Yes. I am."

Such a simple truth.

Grateful people are happy people.

Happy people are generally grateful people.

Ungrateful people are miserable.

From a mental health standpoint, gratitude is good for both heart and mind. Adolescent psychologists recommend that their young patients with anxiety and depression keep a gratitude journal. Adults participating in therapy are often assigned the task of keeping gratitude lists. They find their mental outlook improves.

Gratitude is good for us. Gratitude is biblical.

Hannah thanked God for Samuel (1 Samuel 2). David thanked God for His goodness and for victory (Psalm 54:6–7). Mary thanked God for choosing her to carry the Savior (Luke 1:46–55). The leper thanked Jesus for healing (Luke 17:15–19). Peter was thankful to God for His mercy (1 Peter 1:3). Paul and Silas praised God from prison (Acts 16:25).

Strangely, the more affluent we become, the less grateful we seem to be. Our tendency to overlook our blessings robs us of the joy of gratitude. Fyodor Dostoyevsky once said, "Man only likes to count his troubles but does not count his joys."[8]

I once heard of a man intent on growing in his faith. He hired a counselor to provide him with encouragement and assignments that would move him forward. I can imagine he asked himself many questions. Would his mentor teach him a new prayer technique? Suggest an author to read? Help him to practice his testimony and witnessing strategies?

At the first session, the counselor handed him a blank sheet of paper with these instructions: Find a solitary place and make a list of one hundred things for which you are grateful.

Surprised, and a little irritated, the man went off to complete the task. It took him longer than he expected. When done, he proudly returned the sheet to the counselor. Now, perhaps they would tackle the important stuff.

The counselor thanked him. Then he thrust a second blank sheet of paper into the man's hands. One hundred more.

As he stared at the blank sheet, his agitation grew. But once he started reflecting more deeply on God's unfailing goodness, his annoyance melted away. For the first time, he clearly saw the blessings God had poured out on him day after day. He felt true, worshipful gratitude.

"Give thanks in all circumstances; for this is the will of God in Christ Jesus for you" (1 Thessalonians 5:18).

I want my grandchildren to be happy. I know that grateful people are happy even when the circumstances of life are hard. I pray each grandchild will have a heart of sincere gratitude. I pray they will spend more time counting their joys than their troubles. May the Lord help us all to model gratitude to our grandchildren.

Let us pray that . . .

- our grandchildren will grasp the goodness and generosity of the Lord toward them (James 1:17).

- our grandchildren will freely give thanks to the Lord for His goodness (Psalm 107:1).

- our grandchildren will rejoice and give thanks in every circumstance (1 Thessalonians 5:16–18).

- our grandchildren will walk with the Lord and abound in thanksgiving (Colossians 2:6–7).

- our grandchildren will express gratitude through worship (Psalm 13:6).

- our grandchildren will not fall into the sin of ungratefulness (2 Timothy 3:2).

Heavenly Father, open our eyes to the blessings you give to us in abundance. Give us grateful hearts. As we age, we are tempted to complain. Instead, may your praise, and not our complaints, always be on our lips. Lord, in a world where ingratitude is the norm, we ask you to protect the hearts of our grandchildren from this negativity. Open their eyes to your goodness and love. May they, like the thankful leper, fall at your feet in thanksgiving and worship. Amen.

Think and Do

- Try the twenty-one-day challenge with your grandkids. Let each decorate a notebook for a special gratitude journal. They may not use it every day, but the notebook itself will serve as a reminder to be grateful.
- Small children understand thankfulness. *Thankful* by Eileen Spinelli is a sweet way to remind them to be thankful for the little everyday joys.
- Meditate on Psalm 100:1–5. What is the relationship between thankfulness and worship? Does this psalm create an image in your mind?

"Every good gift and every perfect gift is from above, coming down from the Father of lights, with whom there is no variation or shadow due to change" (James 1:17).

"Oh give thanks to the Lord, for he is good, for his steadfast love endures forever" (Psalm 107:1).

"Rejoice always, pray without ceasing, give thanks in all circumstances; for this is the will of God in Christ Jesus for you" (1 Thessalonians 5:16–18).

"Therefore, as you received Christ Jesus the Lord, so walk in him, rooted and built up in him and established in the faith, just as you were taught, abounding in thanksgiving" (Colossians 2:6–7).

"I will sing to the Lord, because he has dealt bountifully with me" (Psalm 13:6).

"For people will be lovers of self, lovers of money, proud, arrogant, abusive, disobedient to their parents, ungrateful, unholy" (2 Timothy 3:2).

day twelve

The Call of God

When Christ calls a man, he bids him come and die.

Dietrich Bonhoeffer

O God, from my youth you have taught me, and I still proclaim your
wondrous deeds.

Psalm 71:17

In a shady grove on Franklin Graham's dairy farm, a handful of praying farmers and businessmen laid an urgent request before God. They
asked God to send an evangelist to preach the gospel to their city of
Charlotte.

Vernon Patterson, a regular at these meetings, challenged the men
to pray an even more audacious prayer. Could God raise this person
up from their own city?[9]

Six months later, just shy of his sixteenth birthday, Billy Graham
gave his life to Christ. God not only raised up an evangelist from their
own city but from the very farmland on which they had prayed.

Billy pastored his first church at twenty-four. He held his first cru-
sade in Detroit, Michigan, at twenty-nine.

A mission trip to Mexico was the turning point for Jim Elliot. An
architectural student at Wheaton College, Jim had a bright future.
His career path would bring him success and security. God had other
plans. God was calling Jim to take the gospel to unreached people.

In his diary, Jim journaled about his potentially costly decision. "He is no fool who gives what he cannot keep to gain what he cannot lose."[10] Jim Elliot was only twenty-five when he and Pete Fleming—hearts burning to reach the Aucas—arrived in Ecuador.

On January 8, 1956, the Piper Cruiser carrying Jim and his four friends, touched down on a sandy, narrow strip. They hoped to meet members of the Waorani tribes to present them with carefully chosen gifts.

Later that day, along the banks of the Curaray River, the five were killed by the very people they came to reach.

The tragic death of Jim Elliot and his four friends was not in vain. Today, there is a thriving Christian community among the Waorani.

Jim was twenty-eight when his life was taken on that riverbank.

It was approximately 560 BC. Jerusalem was in ruins, thanks to the Babylonians. Young men of good families were carried off to serve the pagan king. Among them were Daniel and three others (whom we know as Shadrach, Meshach, and Abednego). Some historians suggest these young men were only in their mid teens. All went through three years of reeducation in order to serve the king.

The intense efforts to eradicate their Jewish faith and culture were futile. They remained faithful to God in spite of danger. Babylonian authorities issued a malicious edict. Praying to anyone other than the king would be a crime punishable by death. Daniel did not waver in his resolve.

> When Daniel knew that the document had been signed, he went to his house where he had windows in his upper chamber open toward Jerusalem. He got down on his knees three times a day and prayed and gave thanks before his God, as he had done previously. (Daniel 6:10)

God calls young people to serve Him in ways that older people cannot. The energy, courage, and intense commitment of youth fuels life-changing evangelism and discipleship. The future of the church burns brightly when young people respond to God's call to sacrificial service.

Many great missionary movements began with young people answering God's call. If we want to take ground for the kingdom today, the youth of the church are an essential part of this mission.

Many great missionary moments also began with older believers devoted to prayer. Do we dare pray, as did the men in a South Carolina pasture, that God would raise up from our churches, cities, nation—or even our own families—evangelists, missionaries, Bible study leaders, and devoted followers of Jesus? Do we dare ask the Holy Spirit to break through to our grandchildren's generation?

Let us pray that . . .

- we will be in constant prayer for the children and young people in our homes and churches (1 Thessalonians 5:17).
- we will pray for the Lord of the harvest to send out workers (Matthew 9:38).
- we will cheerfully give to the Lord's work and support young people in ministry (2 Corinthians 9:7).
- our grandchildren will hear God's call and say, "Here I am!" (Isaiah 6:8).
- our grandchildren will faithfully serve the Lord (Colossians 3:23–24).
- our grandchildren will not compromise their faith (Acts 5:29).
- our grandchildren will be trustworthy in service (Titus 2:7).

Heavenly Father, we pray that your Spirit would work in the hearts of all our young people. We ask you, the Lord of the harvest, to send laborers. From our grandchildren's generation, raise up Christian servants of integrity and faithfulness. Give our grandchildren hearts to hear your call to serve. Give them the strength of character to resist compromise. Give them a love for your word that will keep them anchored in the truth. May their service bear fruit for future generations and build your kingdom. Amen.

Think and Do

- Young Christians interested in ministry depend on the support of mature believers. Short-term missions, Christian colleges, and camping and youth ministries are vital in preparing young adults for ministry. Ask the Lord how He can use you to encourage and support these efforts.

- Read and meditate on Psalms 146:2 and 92:14–15. Reflect on God's mission for your life today. How can you be an example to the next generation of faithfulness to God's call?

- Our grandchildren need heroes to emulate. Do you have a favorite story of a Christian hero? How did this person's life impact yours? Is it a story you can share with your grandchildren?

"Rejoice always, pray without ceasing" (1 Thessalonians 5:16–17).

"Therefore pray earnestly to the Lord of the harvest to send out laborers into his harvest" (Matthew 9:38).

"Each one must give as he has decided in his heart, not reluctantly or under compulsion, for God loves a cheerful giver" (2 Corinthians 9:7).

"I heard the voice of the Lord saying, 'Whom shall I send, and who will go for us?' Then I said, 'Here I am! Send me'" (Isaiah 6:8).

"Whatever you do, work heartily, as for the Lord and not for men, knowing that from the Lord you will receive the inheritance as your reward. You are serving the Lord Christ" (Colossians 3:23–24).

"We must obey God rather than men" (Acts 5:29).

"Show yourself in all respects to be a model of good works, and in your teaching show integrity, dignity" (Titus 2:7).

day thirteen

Small Things

The great doesn't happen through impulse alone, and is a succession
of little things that are brought together.

Vincent van Gogh

For whoever has despised the day of small things shall rejoice.

Zechariah 4:10

I love northeastern Illinois. Take a drive down any road and you will
see endless cornfields and horse farms. We wait with anticipation for
those spring days when farmers plow the muddy fields, preparing to
plant. Before long, green sprouts dot the earth.

By July, tall stalks wave and rustle in the wind.

Then comes fall. The hum of farm machinery and the glow of
headlights at night tell us harvesttime is here. The air fills with dust
from the dry stalks as corn shoots into waiting trucks. We are amazed
that something that had such a small beginning yields such a harvest.

"The fruit is always present in the seed."[11]

Most of the best things in life start out small. God uses small beginnings to accomplish His purposes. God uses small beginnings in the
lives of our grandchildren to grow their faith.

Jesus used seemingly small beginnings in His ministry. He appointed
a small group of men to spearhead the mission of taking the gospel to
the world. What an unlikely strategy for such an overwhelming job.

You and I are the fruit of that small beginning.

Five barley loaves and two fish—a small boy's lunch, a trivial beginning for a grand feast. "How far will they go among so many?" the disciples asked (John 6:9 NIV). Showing no concern, Jesus multiplied the meager menu. It satisfied a hungry crowd and glorified the Father.

More than once, Jesus used the tiniest of seeds to illustrate kingdom principles.

> The kingdom of heaven is like a grain of mustard seed that a man took and sowed in his field. It is the smallest of all seeds, but when it has grown it is larger than all the garden plants and becomes a tree, so that the birds of the air come and make nests in its branches. (Matthew 13:31–32)

In the most touching example of all, Jesus gathered children (often considered too small to be of any importance) into His arms. "Let the children come to me, and do not hinder them, for the kingdom of God belongs to such as these" (Mark 10:14 NIV).

Great things come from small beginnings.

In Zechariah 4, a servant of God and a civic leader of the Jewish people, Zerubbabel begins the reconstruction of the temple. His faithful efforts yield a small foundation and a simple building. The remaining mountain of rubble overwhelmed the people. Progress on the reconstruction stalled.

Some regarded his work as a failure, a disappointment, as nothing.

God sent the prophet Zechariah to offer words of encouragement to Zerubbabel. "'Not by might nor by power, but by my Spirit,' says the LORD Almighty" (v. 6 NIV). The reconstruction of the temple would not be the result of powerful people doing powerful work. It would be a work of the Spirit of God, the Spirit already at work in faithful Zerubbabel.

Zechariah continued, "The hands of Zerubbabel have laid the foundation of this temple; his hands will also complete it. . . . Who dares despise the day of small things . . . ?" (vv. 9–10 NIV).

Zerubbabel's small beginnings fit perfectly into God's plans.

We are often tempted to dismiss as unimportant the small things we do. Kind words, encouragement, hospitality, sharing Scripture, prayer, or caring for someone in need seems small to us. We even say so. "Oh, it was nothing."

Not true. God honors and multiplies the small things.

We may be discouraged by the big things we cannot offer to our grandkids. Distance, financial realities, or health concerns are obstacles. Let's not despise the small things. Let us instead offer our small beginnings to God. Let us plant our seeds deep and watch for the harvest.

Someone has said, "The day of small things is God's day."

Let us pray that . . .

- our grandchildren will be faithful in the little things God entrusts to them (Luke 16:10).

- our grandchildren will have faith like a mustard seed that will grow and flourish (Matthew 13:32).

- our grandchildren will understand that God uses and values the small and seemingly weak in kingdom service (1 Corinthians 1:25–29).

- our grandchildren will be generous with their small resources and offer them to Jesus (John 6:9).

- we will champion those who are engaged in small beginnings (Zechariah 4:10).

Heavenly Father, thank you for the small things that brought us to you. Encouraging words, verses of Scripture, worship songs that touched our hearts all moved us toward the tipping point. Because of the seeds planted by faithful people, we came to you. Lord, help us not to despise the small things we can do to serve you and our loved ones. Use our small efforts to encourage and inspire. May each small thing we offer help our grandchildren to grow in the grace and knowledge of the Lord Jesus Christ. Multiply our efforts. Help us to take note of and affirm the small beginnings of faith in the lives of our loved ones. Help us to rejoice in any and all growth. Make us faithful in the small things. Amen.

Think and Do

- *The Marvelous Mustard Seed* by Amy-Jill Levine and Sandy Eisenberg Sasso is a wonderful book for four- to eight-year-olds. It will help your grandchild understand the power of that tiny seed. A mustard-seed necklace would be a thoughtful gift for a granddaughter.
- Psalm 139 is a psalm about small beginnings. What small thing has God started in your life recently? Have you noticed small changes or growth in the life of a grandchild? What can you do to reinforce the sacredness of these small and miraculous beginnings?

"Whoever can be trusted with very little can also be trusted with much, and whoever is dishonest with very little will also be dishonest with much" (Luke 16:10 NIV).

"He put another parable before them, saying, 'The kingdom of heaven is like a grain of mustard seed that a man took and sowed in his field. It is the smallest of all seeds, but when it has grown it is larger than all the garden plants and becomes a tree, so that the birds of the air come and make nests in its branches'" (Matthew 13:31–32).

"God chose what is foolish in the world to shame the wise; God chose what is weak in the world to shame the strong; God chose what is low and despised in the world, even things that are not, to bring to nothing things that are, so that no human being might boast in the presence of God" (1 Corinthians 1:27–29).

"Here is a boy with five small barley loaves and two small fish, but how far will they go among so many?" (John 6:9 NIV).

"For whoever has despised the day of small things shall rejoice" (Zechariah 4:10).

day fourteen

Be Content

Actually, only God can satisfy a Christian's heart; man cannot.

Watchman Nee

But godliness with contentment is great gain.

1 Timothy 6:6

Some people collect teapots. Others collect old coins. Children collect rocks, feathers, and acorns. Collections line our shelves. They overflow boxes in our garages. Sometimes our treasures are retired to storage units, making room for new gems.

Famed publishing magnate of the twentieth century, William Randolph Hearst, collected art. The nooks and crannies of his home displayed precious paintings, rare pottery, and graceful sculptures.

Never satisfied with his collection, Mr. Hearst was perpetually in search of more. One painting in particular captured his attention. Repeated attempts to acquire this masterpiece led nowhere. In frustration, he sent a trusted employee on a search for the creation. Imagine the tycoon's surprise when his agent announced it had been found.

Where? The priceless work of art was gathering dust in Hearst's own warehouse. His relentless pursuit of "more" blinded him to the treasure he already possessed.[12]

"He who loves money will not be satisfied with money, nor he who loves wealth with his income; this also is vanity" (Ecclesiastes 5:10).

We always seem to hunger for more. Our appetite for material possessions and power is insatiable. Our relentless pursuit for more blinds us to the treasure we already possess.

The Bible provides an antidote for our hunger for more. It is the biblical virtue of contentment.

In Luke 3, soldiers listened intently to John's preaching on repentance. They questioned him about their own spiritual state. "'And we, what shall we do?' And he said to them, 'Do not extort money from anyone by threats or by false accusation, and be content with your wages" (v. 14).

Soldiers often used coercion and intimidation to line their own pockets. No sane person would challenge the bullying of a soldier. Their gnawing discontent with their wages and low position in life fueled their entitled and destructive behavior.

True repentance would bring a change in both their attitudes and their actions. "Be content with your wages."

Unlike William Randolph Hearst, the contented understand the fleeting nature of wealth and possessions. The truly contented person understands godliness is of greater value than belongings or bank accounts.

"Godliness with contentment is great gain, for we brought nothing into the world, and we cannot take anything out of the world. But if we have food and clothing, with these we will be content" (1 Timothy 6:6–8).

A contented Christian has a peaceful heart even in meager circumstances. He has learned the secret that Paul had learned. "I know what it is to be in need, and I know what it is to have plenty. I have learned the secret of being content in any and every situation, whether well fed or hungry, whether living in plenty or in want. I can do all this through him who gives me strength" (Philippians 4:12–13 NIV).

Jesus is the secret to contentment.

The writer to the Hebrews reaffirms this truth. "Keep your life from love of money, and be content with what you have, for he has said, 'I will never leave you nor forsake you'" (Hebrews 13:5).

Our treasure is not gathering dust in some warehouse. Jesus is our ever-present treasure and our source of satisfaction. No possession rivals the contentment we find in knowing God is always present in our lives. He is our security.

Someone once suggested that the word *leave* in Hebrews 13:5 can be understood as "pull away." God will never pull away from us. He will never remove His loving and supportive presence. We can be perfectly content resting in His presence and provision.

I hope my grandchildren will live comfortable and financially successful lives. But it would break my heart to see them blindly scrambling after money or collecting possessions to satisfy their hungering hearts. I pray their lives will be filled with the peace and contentment that comes from knowing Christ alone.

Jesus is enough.

Let us pray that . . .

- our grandchildren will reject the money trap (Hebrews 13:5).
- our grandchildren will learn to experience contentment in all situations (Philippians 4:11–13).
- our grandchildren will look to Jesus for all their needs (Philippians 4:19).
- our grandchildren will recognize the great treasures they have as believers (Psalm 16:11).
- our grandchildren will be satisfied in their relationship to Jesus (Psalm 17:15).
- our grandchildren will live with eternity in view (Colossians 3:2).
- our grandchildren will give generously to others (Psalm 112:5)

Heavenly Father, we thank you for satisfying the deepest longings of our hearts. Forgive us for the times we foolishly run after money and possessions. We pray that you will protect our grandchildren from the love of money and the discontentment and turmoil it brings. Give them wisdom as they manage their resources. May they give generously

to the work of the kingdom. May they use their financial blessings to bless others. We pray they will find their satisfaction in knowing you. Your love is better than life. Amen.

Think and Do

- Do you know someone who is truly content? What character traits do you see in this person? What can you learn and imitate?

- Generously sharing what we have with others often fosters contentment and gives us a healthier perspective on possessions. Can you volunteer at a food pantry? Provide blankets for a homeless shelter? Buy diapers for a single mom? Sponsor a child through a Christian organization? Involve your grandchildren in one of these projects and watch their attitudes change.

"Keep your life free from love of money, and be content with what you have, for he has said, 'I will never leave you nor forsake you'" (Hebrews 13:5).

"I am not saying this because I am in need, for I have learned to be content whatever the circumstances. I know what it is to be in need, and I know what it is to have plenty. I have learned the secret of being content in any and every situation, whether well fed or hungry, whether living in plenty or in want. I can do all this through him who gives me strength" (Philippians 4:11–13 NIV).

"My God will supply every need of yours according to his riches in glory in Christ Jesus" (Philippians 4:19).

"You make known to me the path of life; in your presence there is fullness of joy; at your right hand are pleasures forevermore" (Psalm 16:11).

"As for me, I shall behold your face in righteousness; when I awake, I shall be satisfied with your likeness" (Psalm 17:15).

"Set your minds on things that are above, not on things that are on earth" (Colossians 3:2).

"Good will come to those who are generous and lend freely; who conduct their affairs with justice" (Psalm 112:5 NIV).

day fifteen

Hardships

Sometimes what we don't want is exactly what we need.
Esphyr Slobodkina and Ann Marie Mulhearn Sayer

And we know that for those who love God all things work together for good, for those who are called according to his purpose.
Romans 8:28

Aleksandr Solzhenitsyn may have been the greatest hero of the twentieth century.

Born in Russia in 1918, Solzhenitsyn was a mathematician and student of philosophy. In World War II, he served as a regiment commander. He received three medals for heroism.

In spite of his contribution to Soviet society, Solzhenitsyn was arrested in 1945. The crime of criticizing Stalin in a private letter earned him eight horrific years in the gulag.

The gulag was brutal. Meager rations, hard labor, and frigid temperatures took a toll on Aleksandr and his fellow prisoners. Many died as a result of the harsh treatment.

After his release, he wrote a novel based upon his experience, *One Day in the Life of Ivan Denisovich*. His writings brought to light the horrors of the gulag and the unbearable injustice of Soviet leadership.

In a final attempt to silence Solzhenitsyn, the Soviet authorities permanently exiled him from his homeland.

His book *The Gulag Archipelago* is considered by many to be the best nonfiction book of the twentieth century. In it he reflected in the most surprising way on the years he spent in the gulag.

> And that is why I turn back to the years of my imprisonment and say, sometimes to the astonishment of those about me: "Bless you, prison!"[13]

The lessons he learned in prison stayed with him until his death. The understanding of good and evil gained from his imprisonment shaped his worldview. The friendships he formed, the faith deepened by suffering, the character he developed, the strength and resilience he experienced were all blessings to his life.

Some historians believe that the work of Solzhenitsyn was the first domino to fall in the collapse of the Soviet Union. Because of the lessons he shared from his gulag years, millions gathered the courage to be free. Bless you, prison, for being in his life.

No matter how large or how small the trial, God cares and can use each one for our good. God uses even the most painful circumstances to bless our lives. But there is more. He uses the lessons we have learned to strengthen and benefit others.

There was another man mistreated and imprisoned unjustly. His name was Joseph. At the end of his story in Genesis 50:20, we see him make a puzzling choice.

He could have chosen anger, revenge, and bitterness toward the brothers who tormented and rejected him. Instead, he made the decision to forgive. He chose to have a heavenly point of view. He declares to his brothers, "You intended to harm me, but God intended it for good to accomplish what is now being done, the saving of many lives" (Genesis 50:20 NIV). Perhaps Joseph would say today, "Bless you, betrayal, rejection, exile, homesickness, and prison, for being in my life."

That God can bring incredible good from suffering is one of the great paradoxes of the Christian faith. That He can bring blessing from pain amazes us. Our finite minds are incapable of understanding.

But it is true. God works for our good. God uses our difficulties to produce character.

We know that for those who love God all things work together for good, for those who are called according to his purpose. (Romans 8:28)

We rejoice in our sufferings, knowing that suffering produces endurance, and endurance produces character, and character produces hope, and hope does not put us to shame, because God's love has been poured into our hearts through the Holy Spirit who has been given to us. (Romans 5:3–5)

Our children and grandchildren will encounter many obstacles and disappointments on their journeys. Losses of all kinds will be woven into their stories. These difficult circumstances can be used by God to increase their faith, build character, and bring blessings to others.

I would climb the highest mountain, swim the deepest sea to keep suffering far from my grandchildren. But that is not possible. Instead, I will pray that God will use the trials of life—both big and small—for their ultimate good. May the Lord enable them to be grateful for even the hard times. May their sorrows shape them into people of great character who lead others to God.

Let us pray that . . .

- our grandchildren will trust God to bring good from their trials (Romans 8:28).

- our grandchildren will believe that what others intend for harm, God intends for good (Genesis 50:20).

- our grandchildren will submit to trials and allow their character to be transformed (Romans 5:3–4).

- our grandchildren will experience God's grace and comfort in trials (1 Peter 5:10).

- our grandchildren will understand that their problems are temporary (Romans 8:18).

- our grandchildren's faith will be steadfast in testing (James 1:2–4).

Heavenly Father, we do not understand how you work hardships to our good, but we believe that you do. We pray you would use our trials as tools for our growth. We pray our grandchildren will learn to trust you through the problems of life. May they have a heavenly perspective on their trials. Give them the endurance to persevere in adversity. Grant them a strong and resilient faith. Use the hard times to strengthen their character and to bring blessings to others. Amen.

Think and Do

- What Joseph may not have understood at the time (the betrayal of his brothers, the deceit of Potiphar's wife) became clear over the years. In hindsight, he could see God's hand. As you look back on past seasons of suffering, where can you see God's hand? How have trials shaped your character? What trial can you now see as a blessing?

- Read and enjoy the story of Joseph with your grandchildren. Children will identify with this biblical hero as they see him overcome his hardships. If you have dress-up clothes, children can reenact the scenes from Joseph's life. Take a few photos and let the children make their own book about Joseph. Children often identify with the character traits of the people they portray.

"We know that for those who love God all things work together for good, for those who are called according to his purpose" (Romans 8:28).

"As for you, you meant evil against me, but God meant it for good, to bring it about that many people should be kept alive, as they are today" (Genesis 50:20).

"Not only that, but we rejoice in our sufferings, knowing that suffering produces endurance, and endurance produces character, and character produces hope" (Romans 5:3–4).

"After you have suffered a little while, the God of all grace, who has called you to his eternal glory in Christ, will himself restore, confirm, strengthen, and establish you" (1 Peter 5:10).

"For I consider that the sufferings of this present time are not worth comparing with the glory that is to be revealed to us" (Romans 8:18).

"Count it all joy, my brothers, when you meet trials of various kinds, for you know that the testing of your faith produces steadfastness. And let steadfastness have its full effect, that you may be perfect and complete, lacking in nothing" (James 1:2–4).

day sixteen

The Name of the Lord

The safest place in the world is in the will of God.

Warren Wiersbe

The name of the LORD is a fortified tower; the righteous run to it and are safe.

Proverbs 18:10 (NIV)

Kings and queens. Lords and ladies. Knights, brandishing gleaming swords while riding noble steeds. As we strolled through the ruins of the fortified city of Carcassonne, we imagined the men and women of medieval times walking the same paths.

The massive city (dating to AD 500) rests on a hill near Aude River in southwestern France. In the evening, the sun transforms the cream-colored stones into explosive pinks and golds. As the sun disappears from the horizon, the main features of the fortress, the fifty-three towers, are like silhouettes against the darkening sky.

For centuries, the towers functioned as the security system for the city. Residents, going about their day or working the fields outside the walls, depended upon tower watchmen to alert them of danger. When the warning sounded, they dropped their tools and ran for the safety of the stronghold.

Climbing uneven, stone stairs to the top, they had a clear view of the coming attack. Perched high above the enemy, the citizens and soldiers had the advantage. The citizens of Carcassonne were famous for raining rocks down upon the heads of their enemies.

These towers offered the citizens the highest degree of security in a city vulnerable to attack.

The writer of Proverbs understood the importance of towers for security and safety. In Proverbs 18:10, he uses the image of a strong tower to describe the safety we find in the name of God. "The name of the LORD is a fortified tower; the righteous run to it and are safe" (NIV).

Our tower, stronghold, refuge, and fortress is the very name of God. Each brick in this strong tower represents a character trait of our God.

When faced with spiritual danger or threats, we drop everything and sprint to our sheltering place. Above the entrance to our strong tower, we see the name of the Lord.

Once inside, we slam and bar the door. Hunkering down in our shelter, we are surrounded by His love, power, wisdom, care, mercy, comfort, holiness, provision, friendship, and deliverance.

We are safely sheltered by His name.

Inside our tower, we gain a fresh perspective on our problems. High in the tower of His name we occupy a superior position. In this place, God sees the coming threats and dangers and protects and fights for us.

An older version of Proverbs 18:10 translates the word *safe* as "set on high."

Trusting in the name of the Lord, we are set on high. We live above the fray. We rise above the circumstances. We remember that God is sovereign, even over trials. He is with us and fights for us. He sets us high above the conflict.

Psalm 27:5 carries a similar theme. "For he will hide me in his shelter in the day of trouble; he will conceal me under the cover of his tent; he will lift me high upon a rock."

In Acts 4:12, Peter reminds us of the power of the name of the Lord. "There is salvation in no one else, for there is no other name under heaven given among men by which we must be saved."

We trust in the name of the Lord for our eternal salvation. He truly is a strong tower. We run to Him and are saved.

The name of the Lord is a precious gift for believers. Let's imagine ourselves running to that tower that bears the name of Jesus above the door. He alone is our safety and security.

I pray that at the hint of danger, our grandchildren will drop everything and run to the strong tower of His name. May they learn to race to Jesus and find safety, security, and salvation.

Let us pray that . . .

- our grandchildren will run to God when attacked (Proverbs 18:10).
- our grandchildren will know God is their refuge and strength (Psalm 46:1).
- our grandchildren will find safety and comfort in the everlasting arms (Deuteronomy 33:27).
- our grandchildren will understand God is their hiding place in times of trouble (Psalm 32:7; 17:8).
- our grandchildren will find salvation in the name of Jesus (Acts 4:12).

Heavenly Father, you are our strong tower. You are our fortress and our rock. You have surrounded and cared for us so many times. Help us to remember you are always there. We pray you will open the eyes of our grandchildren to the safety and peace that your name gives. May they learn early to run to you for safety. We pray they will find great comfort and strength as they meditate on your name. Shelter them. Cover them. Set them high upon a rock, we pray. Amen.

Think and Do

- What young boy can resist stories of knights, kings, and castles? Brandon Hale has written the Prince Martin Epic book series for ages six and up. These books teach boys about bravery, honesty, loyalty, and compassion from a biblical viewpoint. They are written in rhyme, making them more suitable for younger boys.
- In 1 Samuel 19:2, Jonathan instructed David to find a place in the fields or caves to hide from Saul. David was concealing

himself in order to save his life. Read Psalm 32:7. Where is David hiding now? Where was he most secure? Where do you hide in times of trouble?

- Corrie ten Boom and her family lived in Holland during World War II. The story of the courage and faith that motivated them to risk their lives for Jewish neighbors continues to encourage believers today. *The Hiding Place* is a worthy read.

"The name of the LORD is a fortified tower; the righteous run to it and are safe" (Proverbs 18:10 NIV).

"God is our refuge and strength, a very present help in trouble. Therefore we will not fear though the earth gives way, though the mountains be moved into the heart of the sea" (Psalm 46:1–2).

"The eternal God is your dwelling place, and underneath are the everlasting arms" (Deuteronomy 33:27).

"You are a hiding place for me; you preserve me from trouble; you surround me with shouts of deliverance" (Psalm 32:7).

"Keep me as the apple of your eye; hide me in the shadow of your wings" (Psalm 17:8).

"There is salvation in no one else, for there is no other name under heaven given among men by which we must be saved" (Acts 4:12).

day seventeen

The Golden Chain

Kindness is a battlefield.

Shaunti Feldhahn

A man who is kind benefits himself, but a cruel man hurts himself.

Proverbs 11:17

I've read that German literary giant, philosopher, scientist, and states-man Johann Wolfgang von Goethe wrote, "Kindness is the golden chain by which society is bound together."[14]

It is true. Every act of kindness draws people together. Every kind word or deed bonds us and strengthens society.

By contrast, unkindness fractures us. It eats away at marriages, families, neighborhoods, churches, workplaces, communities, and nations. Unkindness is often the first sign of distress when a marriage breaks down. When the golden chain of kindness snaps, we disintegrate.

Small acts of kindness strengthen relationships. Kindness reinforces community.

Delivering a casserole to a new mother, making phone calls to the lonely, pouring a cup of tea for a struggling friend, encouraging the discouraged are acts of kindness that bind us together. It is nearly impossible to separate friends who are bound together by kindness.

Jesus was kind.

Running out of wine at a wedding feast spelled disaster for the embarrassed host. Without wine, the party would come to an awkward end. Hearing of the dilemma, Jesus transformed water into wine of the highest quality. The festivities in Cana went on, all because of the kindness of Jesus.

Jesus saw a grief-stricken widow on her way to bury her only son. He understood the magnitude of her loss. He was aware of the financial hardship it would cause. "When the Lord saw her, his heart went out to her and he said, 'Don't cry'" (Luke 7:13 NIV).

In kindness, Jesus came alongside her in the funeral procession. He offered words of comfort. Then He did the unexpected. He restored her son to her.

The kindness of Jesus toward sinners, children, outcasts, lepers, the sick, the possessed, the repentant, and even His executioners amazes us. If our goal is Christlikeness, we must follow His example of extreme kindness.

Kindness is a virtue. Kindness transforms us.

Kindness benefits both the receiver and the giver. "A man who is kind benefits himself, but a cruel man hurts himself" (Proverbs 11:17).

The New Testament places high value on kindness. In 1 Corinthians 13, as Paul beautifully describes love, kindness is close to the front of the list. "Love is patient and kind" (1 Corinthians 13:4).

In Galatians, kindness is listed as a fruit of the Holy Spirit in our lives. "The fruit of the Spirit is love, joy, peace, patience, kindness, goodness, faithfulness, gentleness, self-control; against such things there is no law" (Galatians 5:22–23).

Kindness is evidence of God at work in our hearts.

Colossians 3:12 commands us to put on kindness like a new set of clothes. It is evidence we are God's chosen ones. "Put on then, as God's chosen ones, holy and beloved, compassionate hearts, kindness, humility, meekness, and patience."

Kindness is worth pursuing. "Whoever pursues righteousness and kindness will find life, righteousness, and honor" (Proverbs 21:21).

Isaiah Champion Jewett's dream of an Olympic medal at the 2020 Olympics was almost a reality. Isaiah was running third in the 800-meter event. Nijel Amos of Botswana was in fourth. Suddenly, in a tangle of arms and legs, both men fell.

Jewett reached over to help Amos to his feet. In a gesture of sportsmanship and kindness, the two men shook hands. Then Jewett draped his arm over Amos's shoulder as they walked to the finish line together. For a brief moment, the golden chain of kindness was visible.

Our world suffers from a kindness deficit. The chain has snapped. We are breaking apart. Blaming, bullying, judging, and slander are the norm.

We need the golden chain of biblical kindness.

Imagine our grandchildren growing up in a kinder world. We each are a link in that golden chain of kindness. May our grandchildren grow to be kind. May their lives reflect the lovingkindness of Jesus.

Let us pray that . . .

- our grandchildren will be led to repentance by God's kindness (Romans 2:4).

- our grandchildren will see God's lovingkindness in their lives (Hosea 11:4).

- our grandchildren will pursue kindness (Proverbs 21:21).

- our grandchildren will be kind and tenderhearted toward others as Jesus is toward them (Ephesians 4:32).

- our grandchildren will clothe themselves in humility and kindness (Colossians 3:12).

- our grandchildren will be kind, even to those who mistreat them (Luke 6:35).

- our grandchildren will have kind, loyal friends (Proverbs 18:24).

Heavenly Father, you drew us to yourself with your kindness. Help us to model the kindness of Jesus to our family, friends, neighbors. Soften our hearts. Enable us to have empathy for those who are hurting. Prompt us to be kind in our actions as well as in our words. May kindness bind our families, our churches, our communities, our nation together once again. We pray our grandchildren will chase after

kindness. Give them tender hearts. May their kindness encourage and comfort others. May their kindness enrich their own lives by strengthening relationships. Help them to be shining examples of the kindness of Jesus. Amen.

Think and Do

- *The Kindness Challenge* by Shaunti Feldhahn helps us gain a better understanding of the power of kindness.
- Kindness and good manners go together. How can we help young people become more polite even with their peers?
- *Always Room for One More* by Sorche Nic Leodhas is a delightful tale of a Scottish family whose generosity and kindness filled their humble home with joy. It will take a little work to read smoothly as it introduces new vocabulary and customs, but it is a sweet example of a community marked by kindness.

"Do you presume on the riches of his kindness and forbearance and patience, not knowing that God's kindness is meant to lead you to repentance?" (Romans 2:4).

"I led them with cords of human kindness, with ties of love" (Hosea 11:4 NIV).

"Whoever pursues righteousness and kindness will find life, righteousness, and honor" (Proverb 21:21).

"Be kind to one another, tenderhearted, forgiving one another, as God in Christ forgave you" (Ephesians 4:32).

"Put on then, as God's chosen ones, holy and beloved, compassionate hearts, kindness, humility, meekness, and patience" (Colossians 3:12).

"Love your enemies, and do good, and lend, expecting nothing in return, and your reward will be great, and you will be sons of the Most High, for he is kind to the ungrateful and the evil" (Luke 6:35).

"A man of many companions may come to ruin, but there is a friend who sticks closer than a brother" (Proverbs 18:24).

day eighteen

At the Pace of the Children

When we are out of sympathy with the young, then I think our work in this world is over.

George MacDonald

I still have many things to say to you; but you cannot bear them now.

John 16:12

In the world of a three-year-old boy, everything is new and delightful. Whether playing with his toy cars, helping Daddy in the yard, or making cookies with Mom, Avett has a spark and enthusiasm that lights up a room.

Our daughter-in-law reports that this little guy has adopted a new phrase. "Wait! Wait! Wait!" Whether it is time for bed, a bath, or dinner, Avett just needs a little more time with his cars, a little more time to snuggle with Mom and Dad, a little more time to be silly.

Have you noticed children move at their own speed? At the precise moment we need to hurry, they shift into slow motion.

In a rush to leave the house? They dawdle. Need to get to Grandma's house for dinner? We wait for a straggler to get to the car. Time for a good-night kiss and lights out? They plead for one more story, and we cannot resist.

Think of how much of each day moms spend moving their children along.

I'm thankful I didn't have Jacob's job. He had an unruly entourage to navigate through difficult terrain. Rachel and Leah and all the children, servants, huge herds, and flocks were under his care and direction. The ambitious plan was to rendezvous with brother Esau at Seir.

In Genesis 33:13–14, Jacob humbly makes a request of Esau. "My lord knows that the children are tender . . . so let my lord go on ahead of his servant, while I move along slowly at the pace of the flocks and herds before me and the pace of the children" (NIV).

Jacob was willing to move at the pace of the children. Was he envisioning little ones with broken sandals that would need repair? Did he imagine hot, tired, and whiny children in need of a rest? Was there a particular slowpoke who came to mind?

It is clear that Jacob considered the needs and the development of his children. He planned ahead. He understood they were tender and that this trip would be draining on them all.

Jacob's request was wise. It would be futile to push the children to move at the pace of the adults. Jacob didn't put the children in charge of the schedule. But he understood their needs were part of the equation.

One of the joys of grandparenting is greater freedom to move at the pace of the children. Our schedules might allow us to spend a few more minutes feeding ducks at the pond. We may feel free to linger at the park as little ones have one more swing.

To move at the pace of children requires compassion. "As a father shows compassion to his children, so the LORD shows compassion to those who fear him" (Psalm 103:13).

Our heavenly Father is in tune with us and our needs. He has compassion on us. In the same way, we can attune ourselves to our grandchildren, their challenges, their needs. We compassionately move at their pace.

Moving at the pace of the children requires gentleness. Jacob's attitude was tender and gentle. Preparing for the journey, how easily he could have been impatient and frustrated at the thought of what lie ahead. Instead, he adopted the outlook of the Good Shepherd.

"He will tend his flock like a shepherd; he will gather the lambs in his arms; he will carry them in his bosom, and gently lead those that are with young" (Isaiah 40:11).

When we move at the pace of the children, we can quickly note when one of our lambs is too weary to go on. It would be useless to insist on hurry. Gathering the tired one in our arms and offering a brief rest may be exactly what is needed.

What applies to the physical needs of our grandchildren applies as well to the spiritual.

Jesus did not hurry the twelve in their spiritual growth. He knew their limits. "I still have many things to say to you, but you cannot bear them now" (John 16:12). His teaching matched their ability to understand. He moved at their pace.

Spiritual growth can be so slow. Our grandchildren need patience, compassion, and gentleness as they mature and flourish—at their own pace.

Children don't always move at a snail's pace. Frequently, we cannot keep up with their antics at the park or their Olympic speeds on a neighborhood walk.

These moments allow us to encourage them to be thoughtful and considerate of others.

Sometimes they need to move at the pace of the grandma.

Let us pray that . . .

- we will find joy in moving at the pace of our grandchildren (Genesis 33:13–14).

- we will humbly consider the needs and limitations of our grandchildren (Philippians 2:4).

- we will resist the temptation to rush the spiritual and moral development of our grandchildren (John 16:12).

- we will guard against impatience that might lead our grandchildren to anger (Ephesians 6:4).

- we will be consistently loving, kind, and patient with our grandchildren (1 Corinthians 13:4).

- we will follow the tender example of our Shepherd in dealing with children (Isaiah 40:11).

- our grandchildren will grow to be thoughtful, considerate people (Philippians 2:3).

Heavenly Father, we thank you for your patience and gentleness. We are grateful you understand our limits and do not push us to grow faster than we are able. Help us to have the same attitude toward our children and grandchildren. Open our eyes to the needs and limitations of each. Help us to show tender love and care for those with health and developmental issues. May our grandchildren learn to exercise patience and thoughtfulness toward others. Amen.

Think and Do

- Some children need more understanding, patience, and care than others. *Bible Promises for Parents of Children with Special Needs* by Amy Mason encourages parents and grandparents who provide care for children with special needs.

- We are often in such a hurry we fail to slow down and enjoy the little moments with our grandchildren. *The World Is Awake* by Linsey Davis (for ages four to eight) will encourage both grandchildren and grandmothers to slow down and remember, "This is the day that the Lord has made; let us rejoice and be glad in it" (Psalm 118:24).

"Let my lord pass on ahead of his servant, and I will lead on slowly, at the pace of the livestock that are ahead of me and at the pace of the children, until I come to my lord in Seir" (Genesis 33:14).

"Let each of you look not only to his own interests, but also to the interests of others" (Philippians 2:4).

"I still have many things to say to you, but you cannot bear them now" (John 16:12).

"Fathers, do not provoke your children to anger but bring them up in the discipline and instruction of the Lord" (Ephesians 6:4).

"Love is patient and kind" (1 Corinthians 13:4).

"He will tend his flock like a shepherd; he will gather the lambs in his arms; he will carry them in his bosom, and gently lead those that are with young" (Isaiah 40:11).

"Do nothing from selfish ambition or conceit, but in humility count others more significant than yourselves" (Philippians 2:3).

day nineteen

Unity

Be united with other Christians. A wall with loose bricks is not good.
The bricks must be cemented together.

Corrie ten Boom

Finally, all of you, have unity of mind, sympathy, brotherly love, a
tender heart, and a humble mind.

1 Peter 3:8

Synchronized swimming was recognized as an Olympic sport in the
1980s. The American team, with their swimming caps and crisp moves,
thrilled our little girls. They created their own routines in our four-
foot pool. Little arms and legs shot out of the water in (near) unison.
After diving under again, their heads popped up for the grand finale
to the cheers and applause of Mom and Dad.

Different ages, different sizes, different abilities, but the girls had
one goal—to synchronize their movements as they imagined standing
on the podium with gold around their necks.

Unity.

Have you ever seen a championship team that excelled while being
divided? In postgame interviews, have you heard a sports drink–soaked,
trophy-holding player credit division and conflict for the win?

The sporting world illustrates for us the beauty and necessity of
unity. It gives us a picture of the power of teamwork. What is true in
that arena holds true in marriages, homes, churches, and communities. Unity helps us to accomplish our goals. It always enriches our
relationships. It brings a joy like nothing else.

"Behold, how good and pleasant it is when brothers dwell in unity!" (Psalm 133:1).

There are few things in life as beautiful as unity. Singing a favorite hymn in unison with other believers, playing on a cohesive team, sharing common ministry goals, lighting a unity candle as bride and groom, praying together as mother and father for our children—some of the best things in life are the result of unity.

Jesus championed unity. On the night before His crucifixion, unity was on His mind.

> The glory that you have given me I have given to them, that they may be one even as we are one, I in them and you in me, that they may become perfectly one, so that the world may know that you sent me and loved them even as you loved me. (John 17:22–23)

This was Jesus's final message to His followers. Clearly, unity was a priority.

To witness to the world of the reality of Christ and to accomplish their goal of taking the gospel to all people, unity would be a necessity.

The disciples had little in common. Peter, Andrew, James, and John were fishermen. Matthew was a tax collector for the Romans, scorned by most Jews. And no one disliked tax collectors more than Simon the Zealot. Zealots were sworn enemies of any Jew who worked with Roman oppressors.

Then came Paul. When he joined the circle, he was a religious leader, scholar, and a recent persecutor of Christians. He was the intellectual of the group. It took a long while for Jewish believers to warm up to this man who was once their enemy and had caused so much fear.

Greeks and Romans joined the Jewish believers. Gentiles hung out with Jews. Believers began to spread the gospel far and wide. Women began to take a more prominent role. From the earliest days, the church was made up of people of different nationalities and languages.

Could such a large group (from different heritages, languages, religious traditions, and experiences) come together? Would they be able to synchronize their activities to accomplish a noble goal?

Yes.

Jesus demolished the dividing wall between each and every group. With no wall to divide them, they became one. "There is neither Jew nor Greek, there is neither slave nor free, there is no male and female, for you are all one in Christ Jesus" (Galatians 3:28).

This group, formerly distanced from one another by heritage and traditions, was united by what they believed. In Ephesians 4, Paul tells us of their shared belief in "one Lord, one faith, one baptism." These beliefs bonded them to one another (v. 5).

In Romans 15, Paul commands believers to live in harmony (synchronize) with each other so "together you may with one voice glorify the God and Father of our Lord Jesus Christ" (v. 6).

Unity was important to Jesus. He was the champion of this important virtue. He not only prayed for it but provided a path to unity.

Unity is a trademark of the church.

In a world that is increasingly fractured, I choose to champion unity. I pray my grandchildren will experience the unparalleled joy of being part of a church. May they enjoy the love and warmth found only in a community of believers. May they synchronize their voices with their brothers and sisters and work to glorify God and fulfill the Great Commission.

Let us pray that . . .

- our grandchildren will be drawn to Jesus as they see the oneness of the church (John 17:20–23).

- our grandchildren will live in unity, as one heart and one mind with other believers (1 Corinthians 1:10; Philippians 2:1–2).

- our grandchildren will love their brothers and sisters and live in perfect harmony (Colossians 3:14).

- our grandchildren will be eager to maintain unity (Ephesians 4:1–3).

- our grandchildren will unite their voices with other believers in praise to God (Romans 15:5–6).

- our grandchildren will live in anticipation of the day when all believers will be unified in worship to God (Revelation 7:9–10).

Heavenly Father, thank you for our brothers and sisters in Christ. We pray you will open our eyes to the importance of living and working together in unity. Forgive us for selfish thoughts and actions which erode unity in our own churches. Unite us as one. May our renewed love and unity be a powerful witness to our broken world. We pray that our grandchildren will live in unity with other believers. May their hearts be filled with agape love. Help them to set aside the self-interests that destroy unity. We pray our grandchildren's generation will champion the cause of unity. Amen.

Think and Do

- Do you remember the worship song, "They'll Know We Are Christians"? This simple 1960s worship song encouraged many young believers during that time. Did it touch your heart? Listen to or read the words of this song again. How can you champion unity in your church?

- Meditate on Colossians 3:14. The word for love here is *agape*. It is a sacrificial, volitional, selfless form of love. How is love the glue that holds us together in unity?

- Even small children can grasp the concept of teamwork. *Swimmy* by Leo Lionni and *Stone Soup* by Marcia Brown entertain and give children a taste of what can be accomplished when we all work together.

"I do not ask for these only, but also for those who will believe in me through their word, that they may all be one, just as you, Father, are in me, and I in you, that they also may be in us, so that the world may believe that you have sent me. The glory that you have given me I have given to them, that they may be one even as we are one, I in them and you in me, that they may become perfectly one, so that the world may know that you sent me and loved them even as you loved me" (John 17:20–23).

"I appeal to you, brothers, by the name of our Lord Jesus Christ, that all of you agree, and that there be no divisions among you, but that you be united in the same mind and the same judgment" (1 Corinthians 1:10).

"If there is any encouragement in Christ, any comfort from love, any participation in the Spirit, any affection and sympathy, complete my joy by being of the same mind, having the same love, being in full accord and of one mind" (Philippians 2:1–2).

"Above all these put on love, which binds everything together in perfect harmony" (Colossians 3:14).

"I, therefore, a prisoner for the Lord, urge you to walk in a manner worthy of the calling to which you have been called, with all humility and gentleness, with patience, bearing with one another in love, eager to maintain the unity of the Spirit in the bond of peace" (Ephesians 4:1–3).

"May the God of endurance and encouragement grant you to live in such harmony with one another, in accord with Christ Jesus, that together you may with one voice glorify the God and Father of our Lord Jesus Christ" (Romans 15:5–6).

"After this I looked, and behold, a great multitude that no one could number, from every nation, from all tribes and peoples and languages, standing before the throne and before the Lamb, clothed in white robes, with palm branches in their hands, and crying out with a loud voice, 'Salvation belongs to our God who sits on the throne, and to the Lamb!'" (Revelation 7:9–10).

day twenty

Spoon, Don't Scoop

You teach what you know but impart who you are.

Jack Frost

They are to teach what is good.

Titus 2:3

"Spoon, don't scoop."

Brushing flour from my hands, I tell Samantha that scooping flour packs it down. "If you scoop," I warn, "the measurement may not be accurate."

Certainly not life-changing advice, but an important hint for those in our family who adore chewy chocolate-chip cookies. Too much flour results in dry cookies. Too little flour and the cookies spread too thin, losing their chewiness.

"Spoon, don't scoop."

When in the kitchen with my girls, I find myself offering tips that others have taught me over the years. I am engaging in an activity embraced by mothers, grandmothers, aunts, sisters, and friends for centuries. We freely share practical advice with one another.

And we love doing it.

The age-old tradition of older women teaching younger women strengthens and supports everyone. Grandma knows how to quiet a fussy baby. Aunt has the best recipe for Thanksgiving stuffing. Sometimes the time spent in the kitchen leads to deeper conversations.

One evening Samantha asked me a question about the Bible. Her inquiry boiled down to this: "How do we know that the Bible is true?" That was an unforgettable moment that began in the kitchen.

I remember with gratitude women who mentored me in both practical and spiritual matters of life. Quite often our conversations began in the kitchen.

Miriam modeled the importance of hospitality as she prepared Sunday lunch for college students. Dorothy modeled the importance of persevering in prayer. Doris knew how to make her home a welcoming place for those in ministry. Nancy exuded a love for God's Word that was contagious and infected everyone she met.

Each woman provided a humble example of a faithful servant.

I often reflect on the advice given to me by these godly women. More often, I think of their character and devotion. They gave much more than encouragement and practical help.

They gave themselves.

Many practical skills can be learned by viewing YouTube videos. We can take online classes or read books. Does this mean personal relationships and mentoring are now obsolete?

No.

Developing discipleship and mentoring relationships has never been more critical. Women are lonely. Adolescents are lonely. Children are lonely. Each needs the encouragement, companionship, and love of others.

The desire for supportive relationships will never fade away. Neither will this command of Scripture. "Teach the older women to be reverent in the way they live, not to be slanderers or addicted to much wine, but to teach what is good. Then they can urge the younger women to love their husbands and children" (Titus 2:3–4 NIV).

There is no end to the good things we can teach our granddaughters and grandsons. Being older doesn't mean we have no influence. In fact, our age is an asset. We have years of experience that give us a deeper well to draw from. Years of walking with God fill us with a desire to share the lessons He has taught us. It is a unique privilege to teach truths that the world no longer values or sees as essential.

Our calling to mentor is a privilege given by God. It is an honor to teach good things to our own grandchildren. Offering them truth that can be tucked away in their hearts for future use fills us with joy. It gives our lives renewed meaning and purpose.

I pray the Lord will help me to be a loving mentor to young Christians, especially within my own family. I also pray that, as He did for me, the Lord will bring faithful men and women into the lives of my grandchildren to encourage them on their journeys.

Let us pray that . . .

- our grandchildren's lives will bear fruit from the truths that we share (Isaiah 55:11).
- our grandchildren will respond to the wisdom of older believers (Proverbs 2:2).
- our grandchildren will someday pass on what they learn from older Christians (2 Timothy 2:2).
- we will grow in integrity and credibility as we serve others (Titus 2:3–5).
- we will speak the truth in loving ways (Ephesians 4:15).
- we will not assume an authoritarian stance over those we serve (1 Peter 5:3).
- we will encourage the exhausted and weak (Isaiah 35:3).

Heavenly Father, you have been so generous to us. Thank you for the many who discipled us in our early days as believers. Their examples of faith and service have set a standard we hope to reach. Help us to pass on their legacy to future generations. Lord, we want to be reverent women filled with integrity. Reveal in us where we need to grow so that we will gain credibility with those we long to serve. Give us willing hearts, ready to teach the good things we find in your Word. Bless our grandchildren with godly mentors. May they take what they learn and someday pass it on to their own children and grandchildren. Amen.

Think and Do

- Do you recall an older woman who mentored you? What words would characterize that relationship? How can you follow her example and keep her influence alive?

- Susan Hunt's *Spiritual Mothering* helps us to focus on the value of older women investing in younger women.

- Do your grandchildren enjoy spending time in the kitchen with Grandma? Lydia Harris has written a cookbook just for you! *In the Kitchen with Grandma* is filled with kid-tested, kid-approved recipes.

"As the rain and the snow come down from heaven and do not return there but water the earth, making it bring forth and sprout, giving seed to the sower and bread to the eater, so shall my word be that goes out from my mouth; it shall not return to me empty, but it shall accomplish that which I purpose, and shall succeed in the thing for which I sent it" (Isaiah 55:10–11).

"Making your ear attentive to wisdom and inclining your heart to understanding" (Proverbs 2:2).

"You then, my child, be strengthened by the grace that is in Christ Jesus, and what you have heard from me in the presence of many witnesses entrust to faithful men, who will be able to teach others also" (2 Timothy 2:1–2).

"Older women likewise are to be reverent in behavior, not slanderers or slaves to much wine. They are to teach what is good, and so train the young women to love their husbands and children, to be self-controlled, pure, working at home, kind, and submissive to their own husbands, that the word of God may not be reviled" (Titus 2:3–5).

"Speaking the truth in love, we are to grow up in every way into him who is the head, into Christ" (Ephesians 4:15).

"I exhort the elders among you, as a fellow elder and a witness of the sufferings of Christ, as well as a partaker in the glory that is going to be revealed: shepherd the flock of God that is among you, exercising oversight, not under compulsion, but willingly, as God would have you; not for shameful gain, but eagerly; not domineering over those in your charge, but being examples to the flock" (1 Peter 5:1–3).

"Strengthen the weak hands, and make firm the feeble knees" (Isaiah 35:3).

day twenty-one

All Roads Lead Home

A housewife's work . . . is surely, in reality, the most important work in the world. . . . Your job is the one for which all others exist.

C. S. Lewis

My people will live in peaceful dwelling places, in secure homes, in undisturbed places of rest.

Isaiah 32:18 (NIV)

Cheryl, the mother of a newborn, was touched when her friend Jen invited her to spend an evening in her home. Sitting side by side on the small couch, they watched the Christmas classic *It's a Wonderful Life*. They snacked, rocked the baby, and laughed as women do.

Thirty years later, Cheryl still recalls the warm welcome of that tiny but loving home. Her weary heart was filled with a sense of belonging. The evening with her friend was exactly what she needed.

I asked my friend what lessons she learned from that one evening so long ago. "Home is more than a place," she answered.

No matter how successful we might be in the eyes of the world, we will always ache for the love and acceptance of home. For some, our own families fulfill that universal longing. For others, friendships or a church community fill that void.

Sadly, for many, finding a nurturing home is a long pursuit marked by stabs of homesickness—a perpetual longing for home.

Home is more than a physical place. Home is where we are encouraged, nurtured, served, and learn to serve in return. At times, it is a shelter. Within its walls we find rest from the demands of the world.

Regardless of our age or life situation—single, married, widowed, divorced, living in a mansion or a one-bedroom apartment—we are all homemakers. Daily we cultivate an atmosphere of love, acceptance, rest, and renewal within the four walls of our home.

Making a home is a noble calling.

God created the first home. He designed it with mankind in mind. "The LORD God planted a garden in Eden, in the east, and there he put the man whom he had formed" (Genesis 2:8).

God elevated the importance of the home and family. He chooses to use the home to fulfill His sacred purposes. "These commandments that I give you today are to be on your hearts. Impress them on your children. Talk about them when you sit at home and when you walk along the road, when you lie down and when you get up" (Deuteronomy 6:6–7 NIV).

I recall hearing author and speaker Edith Schaeffer say that home is where we pass on the baton of faith. Based on Deuteronomy 6, we know this is true.

Sometimes we are dissatisfied with our home. It may not physically suit our needs. But what is more deeply disappointing and heartbreaking is when there are fractured relationships within our families.

Before ascending to heaven, Jesus promised to prepare a new home for us. We will be completely satisfied with the home Jesus is planning. "In my Father's house are many rooms. If it were not so, would I have told you that I go to prepare a place for you? And if I go and prepare a place for you, I will come again and will take you to myself, that where I am you may be also" (John 14:2–3).

A throw pillow here. A colorful rug there. Photos on the mantle. A fridge and pantry stocked with everyone's favorite foods. For the serious homemaker, small gestures and personal touches communicate love and belonging. Every preparation says, "You are welcome here."

Jesus is "making" a home for us. Every preparation is meant to make us welcome.

In our new home, we will spend time with the people we love the most. "I will come again and will take you to myself, that where I am you may be also" (John 14:3). Home is more than a place.

In Genesis, God created the first home. In Revelation, God finally makes His home, His dwelling place, among mankind. "Look, God's home is now among his people! He will live with them, and they will be his people. God himself will be with them" (Revelation 21:3 NLT).

My friend was right. Home is more than a place. Home is where we do life with the people we love. Home is where our faith grows. Home is where we find peace and rest.

Will you join me in praying for our grandchildren's homes? Would you pray for a revival of home and the noble vocation of homemaking? Let us pray for the homeless child who cries out for the loving support of a family.

I pray our homes will become places of warmth and acceptance. May our homes encourage our grandchildren to turn their eyes to their heavenly home.

Let us pray that . . .

- our grandchildren will build their homes with wisdom and understanding (Proverbs 24:3–4).

- our grandchildren will have greater security and peace in their homes (Isaiah 32:18).

- our grandchildren will wisely build up their homes and not tear them down (Proverbs 14:1).

- our grandchildren will focus on the home Jesus is preparing for them (John 14:2).

- our grandchildren will be kind and forgiving in their own homes (Ephesians 4:32).

- we will show hospitality to family, friends, and those in need (Hebrews 13:2; 1 Peter 4:9).

Heavenly Father, oh, how our hearts long for our heavenly home. We look forward to being with you. We ask for your help as we make our earthly homes pleasant places of rest and shelter. May the presence of Jesus be real in our homes. We pray for our grandchildren's homes. May they be filled with the warmth and love of the family. We pray for those in difficult home situations. Bring loving adults into their lives who can demonstrate the love and support a home can provide. When they make their own homes, may they remember that it is you who builds the house. Guide them as they follow your plan for the home and family. May they find in Jesus a safe haven, a refuge, a sanctuary, an eternal home for their hearts. Amen.

Think and Do

- *Hospitality* comes from the same root word that hospital originates from. A hospital is a place of healing. How can you make your home a place of healing by using the gift of hospitality? *Just Open the Door: How One Invitation Can Change a Generation* by Jen Schmidt is a good resource for those new to the concept of Christian hospitality. Browse your favorite Christian book provider for other choices.

- The National Center on Family Homelessness estimates there are 2.5 million homeless children in the United States. This does not include the millions who may have physical shelter but are missing the love and support of one or both parents. How can you pray for and support the families in your church and community?

"By wisdom a house is built, and by understanding it is established; by knowledge the rooms are filled with all precious and pleasant riches" (Proverbs 24:3–4).

"My people will abide in a peaceful habitation, in secure dwellings, and in quiet resting places" (Isaiah 32:18).

"The wisest of women builds her house, but folly with her own hands tears it down" (Proverbs 14:1).

"In my Father's house are many rooms. If it were not so, would I have told you that I go to prepare a place for you? And if I go and prepare a place for you, I will come again and will take you to myself, that where I am you may be also" (John 14:2–3).

"Be kind to one another, tenderhearted, forgiving one another, as God in Christ forgave you" (Ephesians 4:32).

"Do not neglect to show hospitality to strangers, for thereby some have entertained angels unawares" (Hebrews 13:2).

"Show hospitality to one another without grumbling" (1 Peter 4:9).

day twenty-two

A Continual Feast

God bless the good-natured, for they bless everybody else.

Henry Ward Beecher

A cheerful heart is good medicine, but a crushed spirit dries up the bones.

Proverbs 17:22 (NIV)

At the beginning of each year, some Christians choose a word (theme) for the coming months. Their chosen word focuses their efforts on a particular area of needed growth. Someone wants to be more loving. Another believer hopes to grow in grace. Peace is an often-mentioned theme.

If I could return to the beginning of this year, I would choose the word *cheerful*. I want to become a truly cheerful person.

The dictionary defines *cheerfulness* as the state of being noticeably happy and optimistic. Cheerful, good-natured people are enjoyable to be around. They possess a resilient spirit that injects hopefulness into even the most difficult situations.

People are drawn to the cheerful. Their happiness is often contagious. Spending time with the cheerful benefits us body and soul.

The well-known verse in Proverbs encourages this state of mind. "A cheerful heart is good medicine, but a crushed spirit dries up the bones" (Proverbs 17:22 NIV).

We are body and soul. Our moods impact our physical health. A cheerful, hopeful attitude is like swallowing a dose of good medicine. It puts us on the path to healing.

Scientists suggest there is a link between optimism and the immune system. Even a minor family conflict creates enough negativity to dampen the immune response. Health professionals frequently teach patients the importance of maintaining a positive attitude during illness. Cheerfulness is truly good medicine.

Some people tend to be cheerful by nature. Optimism and positivity seem to be in their genes.

Other people lean toward pessimism. Life's bumps and bruises get them down. They would love to be cheerful. They simply do not know how to arrive at that destination.

Can we be joyful, cheerful people even if it is not a familial trait? Is it possible to deliberately nurture this state of mind?

I think so. Here is the secret.

In Philippians 4:4, Paul instructs believers, "Rejoice in the Lord always; again I will say, rejoice." Just four verses later, he reinforces this thought with these words. "Finally, brothers, whatever is true, whatever is honorable, whatever is just, whatever is pure, whatever is lovely, whatever is commendable, if there is any excellence, if there is anything worthy of praise, think about these things" (v. 8).

What we think determines how we feel. What we choose to meditate upon fills us either with negativity or with hope and joy.

A cheerful, optimistic attitude is a result of intentionally thinking about God's goodness to us. Cheerfulness is a choice.

I hope my grandchildren will be cheerful, optimistic people grounded in God's Word. I know their future relationships and careers can be improved by a cheerful spirit or crushed by a negative one. I pray they will experience what the writer of Proverbs 15:15 observed: "the cheerful of heart has a continual feast." May they have cheerful hearts that result in a rich and satisfying life.

Let us pray that . . .

- our grandchildren will desire cheerfulness (Proverbs 17:22).
- our grandchildren will give their negative thoughts to Jesus (2 Corinthians 10:5).

- our grandchildren will rejoice in the Lord always (Philippians 4:4).
- our grandchildren will meditate on God's goodness (Philippians 4:8).
- our grandchildren will refuse to grumble (Philippians 2:14).
- our grandchildren will experience joy as they turn to the Lord for shelter (Psalm 5:11).

Heavenly Father, when we think of all you have done for us, all the good things in our lives, we cannot help but be cheered. Help us to cease negativity and grumbling. May we become pleasant people who can "cheer" on others. Help our grandchildren to see the connection between what they think and how they feel. May they intentionally cultivate an optimistic, faith-filled state of mind. May their hopeful attitude be like good medicine to others. May our grandchildren be encouraged and uplifted each time they cross the threshold of our home. We pray that our entire family will enjoy the continual feast that accompanies a cheerful life. Amen.

Think and Do

- Sometimes I am too serious with the grandkids. Not every conversation needs to be about heavy spiritual issues. Most days we need to be lighthearted. Ecclesiastes 3:4 says that there is "a time to laugh." What can you do to enhance the laughter factor in your home? What games can you play?
- Children (and adults) often overreact to small frustrations. A fun way to help little ones be more optimistic is the book *Every Little Thing*, adapted from Bob Marley's song by his daughter Cedella Marley. The silly song can defuse negativity and bring a smile. Though not a Christian book or song, it is an opportunity to bring up God's care for your grandchildren.

"A cheerful heart is good medicine, but a crushed spirit dries up the bones" (Proverbs 17:22 NIV).

"We destroy arguments and every lofty opinion raised against the knowledge of God, and take every thought captive to obey Christ" (2 Corinthians 10:5).

"Rejoice in the Lord always; again I will say, rejoice" (Philippians 4:4).

"Finally, brothers, whatever is true, whatever is honorable, whatever is just, whatever is pure, whatever is lovely, whatever is commendable, if there is any excellence, if there is anything worthy of praise, think about these things" (Philippians 4:8).

"Do all things without grumbling or disputing" (Philippians 2:14).

"Let all who take refuge in you rejoice; let them ever sing for joy" (Psalm 5:11).

day twenty-three

Terroir
(Tair-wahr)

When you seek stability, trust the gardener to plant you well.
Kathy Carlton Willis

They are planted in the house of the LORD; they flourish in the courts of our God.
Psalm 92:13

Red, ripe, plump, and straight off the vine. Sprinkle a little salt, and let the juice run down your chin. There is nothing quite like a home-grown tomato on a hot summer day.

My father was the king of tomatoes. Wherever he lived, even on a treacherous hillside in Tennessee, his tomato plants flourished. I can still see those staked plants leaning on that grassy hill. He knew just what his tomatoes needed to thrive—even in challenging terrain.

Scripture uses plant life to illustrate the flourishing Christian life. In good or bad terrain, God gives us what we need to flourish. Describing the blessed man, the psalmist writes, "He is like a tree planted by streams of water that yields its fruit in its season, and its leaf does not wither. In all that he does, he prospers" (Psalm 1:3).

The French have an agricultural term that is the secret to a flourishing vineyard—*terroir*. Each vineyard has a distinct terroir. It is made up of a combination of factors that contribute to flourishing vines and delectable wines. The quality of the soil, yearly rainfall, hours of sunlight, humidity, irrigation, choice of grapes, along with the pruning, fertilizing, and devotion of the gardener—all come together to form the terroir. The creation of a fertile terroir does not happen by accident.

My father knew exactly what environment his tomatoes needed to thrive. In the same way, the vineyard owner, gardener, and laborers all know exactly what is needed for the vineyard to flourish. When all factors work together, the result is an abundant, sweet harvest of grapes.

The terroir lends the finished product a one-of-a-kind quality. Swishing and sniffing sommeliers can often tell from which region the wine came because of its distinctive characteristics.

Psalm 1:1–3 reveals the perfect terroir for a flourishing Christian life. It lists the combination of factors that together create a distinctive environment conducive to spiritual growth. It gives us an image of a flourishing and healthy tree that produces fruit at just the right time. We find that spiritual flourishing is no accident.

> Blessed is the man
>   who walks not in the counsel of the wicked,
> nor stands in the way of sinners,
>   nor sits in the seat of scoffers;
> but his delight is in the law of the LORD,
>   and on his law he meditates day and night.
>
> He is like a tree
>   planted by streams of water
> that yields its fruit in its season,
>   and its leaf does not wither.
> In all that he does, he prospers.

Walks not. Nor stands. Nor sits.

The spiritually thriving Christian carefully plants herself in a healthy terroir. She shuns the advice and counsel of those who do not know God. The ungodly are not the source of her wisdom. She rejects worldly philosophies and attitudes. She avoids situations where God is dishonored. As if pulling weeds from a garden, she roots out anything that could hinder spiritual growth.

Instead, the blessed woman sinks her roots into the soil of God's Word. God's law delights her soul. Day and night, she fills her mind with God's truth.

When all these factors of the spiritual terroir work together, the end result is a sweet, abundant harvest of blessing and righteousness. Those around can easily identify the woman as blessed by her unique characteristics. She is fully alive and strong, like a well-watered tree. She does not wither under stress. Her life prospers. She bears fruit that blesses others.

We find the spiritually flourishing Christian again in Psalm 92. This person is planted in the house of the Lord and flourishes in His courts.

> The righteous flourish like the palm tree
>   and grow like a cedar in Lebanon.
> They are planted in the house of the LORD;
>   they flourish in the courts of our God.
> They still bear fruit in old age;
>   they are ever full of sap and green,
> to declare that the LORD is upright;
>   he is my rock, and there is no unrighteousness in him.
>   (vv. 12–15)

They still bear fruit in old age. At a time when one would expect fruit bearing to cease, the flourishing Christian continues to bear fruit. Sometimes the fruit of old age is the sweetest.

I imagine my grandchildren planted in a lush spiritual terroir. The Gardener gives them everything they need to flourish. All the elements are carefully chosen to produce just the right fruit. They courageously root out the weeds of worldly philosophy that threaten to choke out faith. They immerse themselves in God's Word. It is their delight. Their lives are beautiful, blessed, and fruitful all their days.

Let us pray that . . .

- our grandchildren will make the choices that lead to flourishing (Psalms 1; 92:12–15).

- our grandchildren's hearts will be soft, like good and fertile soil (Matthew 13:3–9).

- our grandchildren will choose to let the word of Christ dwell richly in their hearts (Colossians 3:16).

- our grandchildren will root themselves in the wide, long, high, and deep love of God (Ephesians 3:18).
- our grandchildren will grow by God's grace (1 Corinthians 3:7).
- our grandchildren will abide in Christ and bear fruit (John 15:1–10).

Heavenly Father, you are the good Gardener. Thank you for preparing the perfect terroir for our growth. Help us to avoid those things that would stunt our spiritual growth. We will walk not, stand not, and sit not in the ways of the world. We want to bear fruit for you in the autumn and winter seasons. We pray our grandchildren's roots will go deeply into the soil of your love. May your mercy and grace be their nourishment. May your Word, planted in their hearts, grow and bring an abundant harvest. We pray they will each flourish like trees planted by rivers of water. Amen.

Think and Do

- Read John 15:1–10. What can you learn from this passage about flourishing? How would you describe the terroir that brings spiritual fruit?

- Are you a gardener? Share your knowledge with your grandkids by reading *Up in the Garden and Down in the Dirt* by Kate Messner, a look at gardening through the seasons. As a little girl helps in the garden throughout the year, she discovers all that is needed for a truly thriving garden.

"Blessed is the man who walks not in the counsel of the wicked, nor stands in the way of sinners, nor sits in the seat of scoffers; but his delight is in the law of the LORD, and on his law he meditates day and night. He is like a tree planted by streams of water that yields its fruit in its season, and its leaf does not wither. In all that he does, he prospers. The wicked are not so, but are like chaff that the wind drives away" (Psalm 1:1–4).

"The righteous flourish like the palm tree and grow like a cedar in Lebanon. They are planted in the house of the LORD; they flourish in the courts of our God. They still bear fruit in old age; they are ever full of sap and green, to declare that the LORD is upright; he is my rock, and there is no unrighteousness in him" (Psalm 92:12–15).

"He told them many things in parables, saying: 'A sower went out to sow. And as he sowed, some seeds fell along the path, and the birds came and devoured them. Other seeds fell on rocky ground, where they did not have much soil, and immediately they sprang up, since they had no depth of soil, but when the sun rose they were scorched. And since they had no root, they withered away. Other seeds fell among thorns, and the thorns grew up and choked them. Other seeds fell on good soil and produced grain, some a hundredfold, some sixty, some thirty. He who has ears, let him hear'" (Matthew 13:3–9).

"Let the word of Christ dwell in you richly, teaching and admonishing one another in all wisdom, singing psalms and hymns and spiritual songs, with thankfulness in your hearts to God" (Colossians 3:16).

"For this reason I bow my knees before the Father, . . . that according to the riches of his glory he may grant you to be strengthened with power through his Spirit in your inner being, so that Christ may dwell in your hearts through faith—that you, being rooted and grounded in love, may have strength to comprehend with all the saints what is the breadth and length and height and depth, and to know the love of Christ that surpasses knowledge, that you may be filled with all the fullness of God" (Ephesians 3:14, 16–19).

"Neither he who plants nor he who waters is anything, but only God who gives the growth" (1 Corinthians 3:7).

"Abide in me, and I in you. As the branch cannot bear fruit by itself, unless it abides in the vine, neither can you, unless you abide in me. I am the vine; you are the branches. Whoever abides in me and I in him, he it is that bears much fruit, for apart from me you can do nothing" (John 15:4–5).

day twenty-four

Admiration or Adoration

Following Jesus involves losing your life—and finding new life in him.

David Platt

Jesus told his disciples, "If anyone would come after me, let him deny himself and take up his cross and follow me."

Matthew 16:24

Mahatma Gandhi spoke highly of Jesus yet denied His deity. Many world religions esteem Jesus as a profound moral teacher, but they reject His claim to be the Son of God. A fair number of popular media influencers gush sentimental appreciation for Jesus while shelving His most difficult commands.

Jesus has many admirers but few followers.

Admiring Jesus costs little. That is what makes it such an attractive proposition. We sacrifice nothing but gain a sense of self-satisfaction and superiority. We avoid any obligation to obey as we pick and choose which of His teachings feel good to us.

Christian history tells story after story of serious men and women who understood the high cost of following Jesus. All but one of the apostles died a martyr's death. Roman Christians suffered at the hands of corrupt leaders. Chinese Christians have gone underground. Even today, Open Doors reports that each day thirteen Christians die of persecution. Three hundred and nine million more are "living in places with very high or extreme levels of persecution."[15]

These believers, who have sacrificed all, were not admirers of Jesus. They were followers who adored the Lord.

Theologian and philosopher Søren Kierkegaard recognized the sharp contrast between an admirer and a follower. In the hope that his words would revitalize the Christians of his day, he wrote:

> The admirer never makes any true sacrifices. He always plays it safe. Though in word he is inexhaustible about how highly he prizes Christ, he renounces nothing, will not reconstruct his life, and will not let his life express what it is he supposedly admires.[16]

A young woman enjoys the attention of an admirer. An infatuated young man may shower her with compliments and gifts. But if his attentions are self-serving, his charms will soon wear off. He will lose interest. His unwillingness to sacrifice anything for her will cause the relationship to end in disappointment and tears.

In romance, admiration alone is never enough. A lasting relationship depends on the willingness of each person to commit and sacrifice.

In the Christian life, this is even more true. Being an admirer of Jesus is never enough.

To remain as only an admirer of the Lord is self-deception. It can be deadly. "On that day many will say to me, 'Lord, Lord, did we not prophesy in your name, and cast out demons in your name, and do many mighty works in your name?' And then will I declare to them, 'I never knew you; depart from me, you workers of lawlessness'" (Matthew 7:22–23).

Crowds followed Jesus for His healing powers, His authoritative teaching, free lunch, and the hope of an earthly kingdom. Jesus had many admirers.

Had they listened closely, they would have heard, "If anyone would come after me, let him deny himself and take up his cross daily and follow me" (Luke 9:23).

His message was clear. He was calling followers, not admirers.

Today the church needs the same. The world needs humble Christ followers willing to sacrifice all so that the gospel can reach every corner.

I pray we will be true, sacrificial, obedient followers of Jesus. My plea is that the next generation will clearly grasp the difference between appreciating Jesus and truly following Him as Lord. May they know the joy that comes with adoration.

Let us pray that . . .

- our grandchildren will count the cost and give themselves totally to Jesus (Luke 14:28).
- our grandchildren will deny themselves and take up their crosses (Matthew 16:24–25).
- our grandchildren will offer themselves as a sacrifice to the Lord (Romans 12:1).
- our grandchildren will listen for the voice of Jesus and follow Him closely (John 10:4).
- our grandchildren's generation will turn the world upside down by their boldness in following Christ (Acts 17:6).

Heavenly Father, we know the cost is high, but we choose to pay the price of discipleship. Give us clean hands and pure hearts to serve and adore you. Lord, we pray that our grandchildren will answer your call and follow you wholeheartedly. Raise up from their generation devoted Christ followers who turn the world upside down. We pray that the Holy Spirit will strengthen and encourage them as they follow, regardless of the cost. Keep them from the costly error of being admirers instead of followers. Amen.

Think and Do

- For years, millions of believers have been inspired by the stories of Christian heroes. Check your library for the stories of Jim Elliot, Amy Carmichael, Corrie ten Boom, Hudson Taylor, Eric Liddell, and others. There are children's versions for many of these heroes' stories. For your own reading, the Voice of the Martyrs' website contains useful information.

- Read Matthew 7:23–28. Jesus makes it clear that there will be false prophets (admirers) who will claim to be followers. Despite their works, their hearts do not belong to Him. Verses 24–25 reveal the key to crossing the line from admirer to follower. What does this mean for your life? For the lives of your grandchildren?

"Which of you, desiring to build a tower, does not first sit down and count the cost, whether he has enough to complete it?" (Luke 14:28).

"Jesus told his disciples, 'If anyone would come after me, let him deny himself and take up his cross and follow me. For whoever would save his life will lose it, but whoever loses his life for my sake will find it. For what will it profit a man if he gains the whole world and forfeits his soul? Or what shall a man give in return for his soul?'" (Matthew 16:24–26).

"I appeal to you therefore, brothers, by the mercies of God, to present your bodies as a living sacrifice, holy and acceptable to God, which is your spiritual worship" (Romans 12:1).

"When he has brought out all his own, he goes before them, and the sheep follow him, for they know his voice" (John 10:4).

"They dragged Jason and some of the brothers before the city authorities, shouting, 'These men who have turned the world upside down have come here also'" (Acts 17:6).

day twenty-five

Is Anyone Listening?

Prayer delights God's ears: it melts his heart.
Thomas Watson

Truly God has listened; he has attended to the voice of my prayer.
Psalm 66:19

Do you ever feel as if no one is listening?

Some days even our family's smart device ignores me. A recent request for Alexa to play Christmas music went awry. Instead of the peaceful strains of "Away in a Manger," the house rocked with hip-hop music.

I wonder, Am I speaking a different language? Am I saying too much? Too little? The women in our family are soft-spoken and occasionally feel unheard. Maybe it is in the genes.

Years ago, a head cold made it difficult for me to hear my five-year-old granddaughter, Nicole. Finally, I sat on the floor next to her. I tilted my head and turned one ear her way. I wanted to catch every word. I wanted her to know I cared and I was listening.

Immediately, like a gentle whisper, God spoke to my heart as I remembered a verse from Psalms. "I turn my ear to you."

Just as I had moved closer and turned my ear toward Nicole, God leans toward me and catches every word. He does not miss a syllable.

He loves and listens.

In Psalm 116:2, the psalmist wrote, "Because he inclined his ear to me, therefore I will call on him as long as I live." Amazed and humbled that God listened so intently and personally, the psalmist made a commitment to a lifetime of prayer.

It seems God not only listens, but His listening is intentional and focused. The act of turning toward a person symbolizes an eagerness, a desire to hear every detail of what they say. When someone turns their ear toward us, it is because we are valued.

God values our every plea.

When self-pity whispers that no one is listening, I remember the whisper I heard so many years ago. God is listening. He has inclined His ear to me.

The listening God is an answering God. "Before they call I will answer; while they are yet speaking I will hear" (Isaiah 65:24).

He will answer our prayers in the best way at the best time.

Sometimes our task is to wait on the answering God. "As for me, I will look to the LORD; I will wait for the God of my salvation; *my God will hear me*" (Micah 7:7, emphasis added).

He is a listening God. He is an answering God. He is a God who remembers.

Scripture teaches that God remembers His covenant of love for a thousand generations. He certainly remembered the groanings of His suffering people in Egypt. He said He engraved Israel's name on His hand as a sign that He does not forget His children. He remembers our tears and our sighs. He remembers and fulfills every promise.

To our joy and awe, Revelation 5:8 tells us He remembers, preserves, and delights in our prayers. "When he took the scroll, the four living beings and the twenty-four elders fell down before the Lamb. Each one had a harp, and they held gold bowls filled with incense, which are the prayers of God's people" (NLT).

Our prayers are precious to God. Each prayer is as pleasing to Him as fragrant incense. Our prayers are never lost or far from His sight.

In the words of a great man of prayer, E. M. Bounds, "God shapes the world by prayer. Prayers are deathless. . . . Prayers outlive the lives of those who uttered them; outlive a generation, outlive an age, outlive a world."[17]

God hears your prayers on behalf of your grandchildren. Even now, He is leaning in, waiting to hear the whispers of your heart. He treasures every sincere and tearful plea. You can be confident He will remember and guard your prayers.

Our grandchildren will have days when they lament, "No one listens to me." I pray they will be comforted when we turn toward them and whisper, "God is listening."

Let us pray that . . .

- our grandchildren will be confident that God intentionally hears their prayers (Psalm 116:2).
- our grandchildren will not harbor sin that will hinder their prayer lives (Psalm 66:18).
- our grandchildren will know God hears when they pray according to His will (1 John 5:14).
- our grandchildren will understand God sometimes answers prayers in unexpected ways (Isaiah 55:8–9).
- our grandchildren will abide in Christ and have effective prayer lives (John 15:7).
- our grandchildren will always pray and never give up (Luke 18:1).

Heavenly Father, our hearts fill with joy, knowing that you incline your ear to us. Thank you for your promise to hear and answer. Thank you for treasuring our heartfelt prayers. We pray our grandchildren will believe that you are ready to hear their prayers. May they be comforted knowing you lean in to hear their requests. May they find great delight in knowing you are near. Amen.

Think and Do

- Author Tricia Goyer has written a book on prayer for children. *Prayers That Changed History* is a collection of twenty-five inspirational stories. Because it's written for ages eight and up, you may find that some stories are too intense for a sensitive eight-year-old but inspiring and encouraging for older children.

- "Let's pray about it." Every grandchild needs to hear those words. When we pray for their immediate need, we are showing our grandchild that we hear and so does God. How can you gently incorporate more prayer into the life of your family? You may become your grandchild's prayer partner.

"Because he inclined his ear to me, therefore I will call on him as long as I live" (Psalm 116:2).

"If I had cherished iniquity in my heart, the Lord would not have listened" (Psalm 66:18).

"This is the confidence that we have toward him, that if we ask anything according to his will he hears us" (1 John 5:14).

"My thoughts are not your thoughts, neither are your ways my ways, declares the LORD. For as the heavens are higher than the earth, so are my ways higher than your ways and my thoughts than your thoughts" (Isaiah 55:8–9).

"If you abide in me, and my words abide in you, ask whatever you wish, and it will be done for you" (John 15:7).

"He told them a parable to the effect that they ought always to pray and not lose heart" (Luke 18:1).

day twenty-six

Christmas Peace

I heard the bells on Christmas Day
Their old, familiar carols play,
And wild and sweet, the words repeat
Of peace on earth, goodwill to men.

Henry Wadsworth Longfellow

Glory to God in the highest, and on earth peace among those with whom he is pleased!

Luke 2:14

On Christmas Eve, thousands gather in the Old Great Square of Turku, Finland. Small fires glow to celebrate the occasion and warm the crowd. In quiet expectation, citizens look toward the balcony of Brinkkala Manor, the historic town hall.

A men's choir, elegant in black coats, hats, and white neck scarves, sings, "A Mighty Fortress Is Our God." As the clock strikes twelve noon, french doors open. A solemn government official appears on the balcony to make the Declaration of Christmas Peace, a tradition that began in the early 1300s.

Unrolling the parchment, he reads, "Tomorrow, God willing, is the graceful celebration of the birth of our Lord and Saviour; and thus is declared a peaceful Christmas time to all, by advising devotion and to behave otherwise quietly and peacefully."[18] The Declaration concludes with a reminder of the grave consequences to any who violate the Christmas peace.

Christmas peace has been declared.

Instantly, public transportation comes to a standstill. Shops close. Businesses turn out the lights. Streets are quiet—no hustle, no bustle. Everyone scurries home to saunas, family gatherings, and Christmas Eve dinners. And woe to the careless soul who breaks this sacred peace.

Each Christmas, our hearts are drawn to the baby sleeping peacefully in the manger. Every scene from the nativity communicates peace as we celebrate and worship the Prince of Peace.

The first declaration of Christmas peace was not made in Finland, but in a shepherd's field on a starry night. "Glory to God in the highest, and on earth peace among those with whom he is pleased" (Luke 2:14).

Jesus made His own declaration of peace, not from a balcony, not in a shepherds' field, but as He sat with His disciples the night before His death. In the quiet of the upper room, He presented them with a parting gift. "Peace I leave with you; my peace I give to you. Not as the world gives do I give to you" (John 14:27).

What a declaration!

Jesus didn't promise His friends an easy life with no problems. He didn't guarantee a life free of conflict. He promised a peace unlike any the world had ever known.

At best, the world's peace is fragile and fleeting. Worldly peace can evaporate in a moment. It is determined by changing external circumstances.

Even now, there are nations violating peace treaties. Agreements easily made can be just as easily cast aside. Millions of souls desperately long for just one moment of peace.

The prophet Jeremiah condemned those who carelessly promised worldly peace. "They have healed the wound of my people lightly, saying, 'Peace, peace,' when there is no peace" (Jeremiah 8:11). The peace declared by these leaders was wishful thinking, a sham, a cruel gesture.

The peace Jesus offers is enduring and eternal. It is not dependent upon circumstances. Knowing Jesus loves and cares for us brings a calmness to our souls. We have peace because we know that God is loving, sovereign, and powerful.

The peace Jesus offers did not come easily. It was purchased at great cost. "In him all the fullness of God was pleased to dwell, and through him to reconcile to himself all things, whether on earth or in heaven, making peace by the blood of his cross" (Colossians 1:19–20).

Isaiah 26:3 gives us a key to experiencing the perfect peace that Jesus promises. "You keep in perfect peace all who trust in you, all whose thoughts are fixed on you" (NLT). This believer rivets her thoughts on God. Because of her complete trust in God's faithfulness and goodness, she is steady, stable, and at peace.

God's promise of peace to believers will never be revoked.

"'The mountains may depart and the hills be removed, but my steadfast love shall not depart from you, and *my covenant of peace shall not be removed*,' says the LORD, who has compassion on you" (Isaiah 54:10, emphasis added).

Our grandchildren are living in a world of conflict and turmoil, a world without peace. At Christmas, they catch a glimpse of the peace promised by angels. Their hearts are stilled as they stand by the cradle of the Prince of Peace. Candlelight and Christmas hymns lead them to precious moments of quiet.

I want more for them than a few moments of peace as they gather around a Christmas tree or sing Christmas carols. I long for each one to know peace "at all times in every way" (2 Thessalonians 3:16). This peace comes only from knowing the Lord of peace.

When our sins separated us from God, making us enemies, Jesus came to put an end to the conflict. He wiped our slate clean and restored our relationship to the Father.

How will our grandchildren receive this lasting peace? By faith in the Lord Jesus Christ. "Therefore, since we have been justified by faith, we have peace with God through our Lord Jesus Christ" (Romans 5:1).

Jesus is our peace. His death on the cross was sufficient.

It is fitting that we should celebrate the birth of the Savior with a Declaration of Peace. To know and love Jesus is to know His peace—at Christmas and all year long.

May our grandchildren know Him, love Him, place their faith in Him, and receive the enduring peace declared by angels.

Let us pray that . . .

- our grandchildren will let the peace of Christ rule their hearts (Colossians 3:15).

- our grandchildren will receive the peace Jesus offers and find tranquility in the midst of troubles (John 14:27).

- our grandchildren will experience peace as they reflect on the birth of the Prince of Peace (Luke 2:14).

- our grandchildren will have the peace that comes from being justified by Christ (Romans 5:1).

- our grandchildren will fix their eyes on God and be kept in peace (Isaiah 26:3).

- our grandchildren will respect, esteem, and live at peace with others (1 Thessalonians 5:12–13).

- our grandchildren will replace worry with prayer and be filled with the peace of God that surpasses understanding (Philippians 4:6–7).

Heavenly Father, thank you for the birth of the Prince of Peace. Let His peace rule in our hearts. Thank you for those quiet Christmas moments that give us a taste of your sweet peace. May your perfect peace melt away our anxiety, anger, bitterness, and unforgiveness. We pray our homes will be loving and peaceful. May our grandchildren experience the deep peace that comes from knowing Jesus. We pray our grandchildren will rivet their thoughts on Jesus and experience His perfect peace. Amen.

Think and Do

- The Declaration of Christmas Peace can be watched via livestream from Finland on Christmas Eve.

- *'Twas the Evening of Christmas* by Glenys Nellist is a beautifully illustrated telling of the Christmas story. Using the pattern and rhythm of Clement Moore's *'Twas the Night Before Christmas*, Nellist's book will be a great addition to your Christmas readings.

- Do you long for peace during the holiday season? What disturbs your peace? What truths nurture your peace at Christmas and all year long?

"Let the peace of Christ rule in your hearts, to which indeed you were called in one body. And be thankful" (Colossians 3:15).

"Peace I leave with you; my peace I give to you. Not as the world gives do I give to you. Let not your hearts be troubled, neither let them be afraid" (John 14:27).

"Glory to God in the highest, and on earth peace among those with whom he is pleased!" (Luke 2:14).

"Therefore, since we have been justified by faith, we have peace with God through our Lord Jesus Christ" (Romans 5:1).

"You keep him in perfect peace whose mind is stayed on you, because he trusts in you" (Isaiah 26:3).

"We ask you, brothers, to respect those who labor among you and are over you in the Lord and admonish you, and to esteem them very highly in love because of their work. Be at peace among yourselves" (1 Thessalonians 5:12–13).

"Do not be anxious about anything, but in everything by prayer and supplication with thanksgiving let your requests be made known to God. And the peace of God, which surpasses all understanding, will guard your hearts and your minds in Christ Jesus" (Philippians 4:6–7).

day twenty-seven

God's Outstretched Hand

God wants to give us something, but cannot, because our hands are full—there's nowhere for Him to put it.

Augustine

For I am the LORD your God who takes hold of your right hand and says to you, Do not fear; I will help you.

Isaiah 41:13 (NIV)

A mother reaches for a toddler's hand as they cross the street. A young couple strolls through a park, fingers intertwined and oblivious to the world. A newborn wraps his tiny fingers around Dad's as they meet for the first time. A son sits at his father's bedside, stroking a frail hand in a final goodbye.

Holding hands. This simple act communicates our desire to protect, guide, support, reassure, and help. It is an intimate gesture that connects us to each other.

Sometimes we hold hands to gather strength from one another.

In her last years, my grandmother was often shaky. If we reached out to steady her, she implored, "Just hold my hand." She found strength in knowing someone was holding on to her.

Did you know God reaches for your hand?

In Isaiah 41, the prophet had a mixed message for God's people. They were going to experience difficult times as well as seasons of redemption and victory. Verse 13 reassured them of God's plan to get them through either situation: "I am the LORD your God who takes hold of your right hand and says to you, Do not fear, I will help you" (NIV).

Most people are right-handed. In Scripture, the right hand symbolizes a person's source of strength. God promised to take His people by their right hand; He would strengthen them, steady them, support them. When their strength wavered, God would give them His strength. "Do not fear; I will help you."

This intimate gesture was a sign of God's love, care, and power.

In Psalm 77, the psalmist cries out to God. Asaph's pleadings were persistent and desperate. Yet God did not answer. Troubled and in anguish, Asaph refused to be comforted. Had God abandoned him? Would God never answer and bring justice? "Has God forgotten to be gracious? Has he in anger shut up his compassion?" (v. 9).

Determined to make sense of his troubles, Asaph chose to remember God's faithfulness in the past. "Then I thought, 'To this I will appeal: the years when the Most High *stretched out his right hand.* I will remember the deeds of the LORD; yes, I will remember your miracles of long ago" (vv. 10–11 NIV, emphasis added).

Asaph recalled the times God stretched out His right hand (signifying His strength). Time after time He helped, protected, and saved His people. Fear and anguish melted away as Asaph recalled the love, power, and strength of God's right hand in the past. If God had reached out before, He could be trusted to do so again.

The image of God's outstretched hand is a source of comfort to me. When in need (and if I am willing), He takes me by the hand and whispers, "Do not fear; I will help you" (Isaiah 41:13 NIV).

As I think of God stretching out His hand to help me, I am inspired to stretch out my hand to help and encourage others. "Beloved, if God so loved us, we also ought to love one another" (1 John 4:11).

We won't always be there to hold our grandchildren's hands. It comforts us to know that God is ready and willing to take them by the hand. He will strengthen their right hand. He will come to their aid. I pray they will allow God to take them by the hand to gently lead, protect, and save.

Let us pray that . . .

- our grandchildren will know that God can strengthen them in every situation (Philippians 4:13).

- our grandchildren will draw near to God to find strength (Hebrews 4:16).

- our grandchildren will believe that God's hand can reach any situation if we are willing to follow Him (Isaiah 59:1).

- our grandchildren will know that their help comes from the Maker of heaven and earth (Psalm 121:2).

- our grandchildren will seek the Lord's strength and presence continually (1 Chronicles 16:11).

- our grandchildren will trust in the right hand of the Lord to care for them wherever they are (Psalm 139:10).

Heavenly Father, our souls are comforted by the image of you reaching out to strengthen, steady, and save us. Help us to reach out to strengthen and steady others. We pray our grandchildren will embrace the truth that you are always ready to come to their aid. May their hearts be warmed at the thought of your righteous right hand stretching out to save them. May they never hesitate to cry out to you, "Just hold my hand." We praise you for the years of your outstretched hand. Amen.

Think and Do

- Want to help your little ones reach out to God? *God Gave Us Prayer* by Lisa Tawn Bergren will help your littlest grandchild know that God loves them and hears their prayers.

- When has God reached out to steady and save you? If you journal, spend a few moments writing about one of those experiences.

"I can do all things through him who strengthens me" (Philippians 4:13).

"Let us then with confidence draw near to the throne of grace, that we may receive mercy and find grace to help in time of need" (Hebrews 4:16).

"Behold, the LORD's hand is not shortened, that it cannot save, or his ear dull, that it cannot hear" (Isaiah 59:1).

"My help comes from the LORD, who made heaven and earth" (Psalm 121:2).

"Seek the LORD and his strength; seek his presence continually!" (1 Chronicles 16:11).

"If I take the wings of the morning and dwell in the uttermost parts of the sea, even there your hand shall lead me, and your right hand shall hold me" (Psalm 139:9–10).

day twenty-eight

I'm a Believer

I believe in Christianity as I believe that the Sun has risen, not only because I see it but because by it, I see everything else.

C. S. Lewis

Blessed are those who have not seen and yet have believed.

John 20:29

Down every aisle of my favorite craft store, I am greeted by wall hangings, table décor, and posters bearing one familiar word, *believe*. Big-box and home stores follow the same trend. We are constantly being encouraged to "believe."

Believe in what, I ask? Believe in yourself? Believe in your dreams? Believe everything is going to be all right? Believe in Christmas magic?

Our beliefs determine who we are and how we behave. Beliefs shape our friendships, worldviews, and futures. Our beliefs either give us strength or leave us broken.

The size of the crowds exploded after Jesus fed the five thousand. They followed Him everywhere. They clamored for more miracles. Instead of fulfilling their request, Jesus offered to satisfy their spiritual hunger.

With miracles and food on their minds, they came to Jesus looking for answers. "What must we do to do the works God requires?" (John 6:28 NIV).

Were they asking what works they needed to do in order to be saved? Or did they believe that to please God one must do miracles like Jesus?

Jesus answered, "The work of God is this: to believe in the one he has sent" (v. 29 NIV).

The work (singular) of God precedes all other works (plural).

God's desire for them, the work He wanted them to do, was simply to believe in Jesus. Belief was the ultimate purpose of each miracle. Moving unbelievers toward belief was the goal.

Belief was the key that would unlock the door. Once they stepped over the threshold of belief, everything in life would change.

The words of Jesus found in the Gospel, reveal the priority of belief.

Everyone who lives and believes in me shall never die. Do you believe this? (John 11:26)

Jesus said to him, "Have you believed because you have seen me? Blessed are those who have not seen and yet have believed." (John 20:29)

For this is the will of my Father, that everyone who looks on the Son and believes in him should have eternal life. (John 6:40)

Whoever believes in him is not condemned, but whoever does not believe is condemned already, because he has not believed in the name of the only Son of God. (John 3:18)

For God so loved the world, that he gave his only Son, that whoever believes in him should not perish but have eternal life. (John 3:16)

The world is not shy about telling us what to believe. Secular philosophies and faulty thinking daily threaten to creep into our lives. Faith in Jesus is mocked and ridiculed. If this is difficult for us, imagine the challenge it is to our grandchildren.

We must know what we believe and be unafraid to share our beliefs when we can.

I pray my grandchildren will believe in Jesus. I pray they will have a firm foundation of faith that is unshakable. Join me in praying for a revival of belief in their generation.

Let us pray that . . .

- our grandchildren will be drawn to Jesus by the work of the Father (John 6:44).
- our grandchildren will believe in Jesus even though they have never seen Him (John 20:29).
- our grandchildren will believe in Jesus and receive eternal life (John 6:47; 3:16).
- our grandchildren will believe that Jesus is the Son of God and become overcomers (1 John 5:5).
- our grandchildren's faith will please God (Hebrews 11:6).
- our grandchildren will believe in Jesus at all times (John 14:1).

Heavenly Father, we thank you for the day we believed and stepped into a brand-new life. We pray that your Holy Spirit would draw our grandchildren to Jesus and to belief in Him. Even though they have never seen you, may they experience the blessedness of believing. May we always remember that belief precedes work. Help us to know that the priority is always the same—to believe in the One you have sent. Amen.

Think and Do

- Many Christian retailers carry art, plaques, and wall hangings. Displaying your beliefs (the Ten Commandments, the Lord's Prayer) allows you to share God's truth with grandchildren without saying a word.
- When did you first believe? Do you remember the events that led up to that moment? Meditate on Romans 13:11. What encouragement does it bring?

"No one can come to me unless the Father who sent me draws him. And I will raise him up on the last day" (John 6:44).

"Jesus said to him, 'Have you believed because you have seen me? Blessed are those who have not seen and yet have believed'" (John 20:29).

"Truly, truly, I say to you, whoever believes has eternal life" (John 6:47).

"For God so loved the world, that he gave his only Son, that whoever believes in him should not perish but have eternal life" (John 3:16).

"Who is it that overcomes the world except the one who believes that Jesus is the Son of God?" (1 John 5:5).

"Without faith it is impossible to please him, for whoever would draw near to God must believe that he exists and that he rewards those who seek him" (Hebrews 11:6).

"Let not your hearts be troubled. Believe in God; believe also in me" (John 14:1).

day twenty-nine

The Upper Room

Living communion with God in which He is real, alive, fresh, and present to your soul energizes a God-centered life.

Colin S. Smith

Jesus answered him, "If anyone loves me, he will keep my word, and my Father will love him, and we will come to him and make our home with him."

John 14:23

Scattered throughout Jerusalem, large open rooms in the upper level of homes provided Jewish pilgrims a place to gather for the Feast of the Passover. Jesus and His disciples shared this sacred meal in just such an upper room.

Imagine the glow and smell of oil lamps, the simple furniture, the traditional food.

Up till now most of Jesus's ministry was public. This night His attention was focused on twelve men.

This was a private event.

Have you ever imagined yourself quietly sitting with Jesus in this upper room? Just to be in His presence fills you with joy and peace. You drink in every precious, life-giving word. You hear affection in His voice as He calls those assembled His "friends."

What I wouldn't give for an hour with Jesus in the upper room. Of course, that is not possible physically. But in my spiritual life, I can make choices that nurture and deepen my relationship with the Savior, that bring me into His presence.

In his book, *The Safest Place on Earth*, author and counselor Larry Crabb uses the upper room as a metaphor for a life lived in the Spirit. He devotes much of his book to encouraging people to stay in the upper room of their hearts.[19]

For the disciples, the upper room was the place where they experienced Christ's love, heard His teaching, and sat in His presence. For us, the upper room can be the place in our hearts where we enjoy His presence as well, where we are spiritually alive and surrendered to the Spirit.

Jesus knew when the Passover meal ended He would be leaving His disciples. Perhaps the men sensed the coming loss. They knew they would eventually leave that upper room. The nearness they now experienced would soon be gone.

But as Jesus gave final instructions to these men He deeply loved, He told them how they could remain in the upper room spiritually. He told them to "abide." He gave the command not once, not twice, but three times.

Abide in Christ. "Abide in me, and I in you. As the branch cannot bear fruit by itself, unless it abides in the vine, neither can you, unless you abide in me" (John 15:4). In other translations, the word *remain* is used instead of *abide*. Both words imply a permanent, close connection between us and Christ.

Abiding and remaining both require "staying put." When we abide in Christ, we intentionally stay close to Him.

Abide in His Word. "If you abide in me, and my words abide in you, ask whatever you wish, and it will be done for you" (v. 7). Abiding and remaining in God's Word is not only about reading Scripture. When we remain in God's Word, and God's Word remains in us, we internalize the absolute truth. The truth finds a permanent place in our hearts.

Abiding and remaining in God's Word requires "staying put" when worldly philosophies threaten to drag us under.

Abide in His love. "As the Father has loved me, so have I loved you. Abide in my love. If you keep my commandments, you will abide in my love, just as I have kept my Father's commandments and abide in his love" (vv. 9–10).

When we abide in His love, we do not wander off looking for other, lesser loves. We stay close to the One who loves us.

The disciples would not commune with Jesus in that upper room again. But if they took to heart His teaching and remained in Him, they would still know His presence.

When my spiritual life feels dry and strained, it would be wonderful to sit with Jesus. Until that is possible, I will remind myself to go back to (and stay put in) the upper room of my heart where Jesus abides and where I am spiritually alive. When I draw near to Him once again, I know He will draw near to me (James 4:8).

Can you think of any greater experience for your grandchildren than abiding in Christ and knowing His love? I pray my grandchildren will focus on Jesus and abide in Him. May they stay in the upper room of their hearts where Jesus dwells. May they stay close to the One who loves them.

Let us pray that . . .

- our grandchildren's daily walk will be evidence of abiding in Christ (1 John 2:6).

- our grandchildren will abide in Christ until He returns (1 John 2:28).

- our grandchildren will abide in Christ's word as true disciples (John 8:31).

- our grandchildren will reject sin by abiding in Christ (1 John 3:6).

- our grandchildren will have the Spirit as a sign of abiding in Christ (1 John 4:13).

- our grandchildren will draw near to God (James 4:8).

- our grandchildren will stay in the upper room of their hearts through keeping in step with the Spirit (Galatians 5:25).

Heavenly Father, how we would love to sit with Jesus. Until we are with you in your kingdom, we choose to abide in Christ and remain in your Word. Forgive us for the things that distract us and pull us away. We will stay put. It is our heart's desire that each of our grandchildren would stay close to you. May they enjoy sweet communion with Jesus in the upper room of their hearts. We pray they will abide in your love all the days of their lives. May we all stay close to Christ and bear fruit for the kingdom. Amen.

Think and Do

- Are you looking for a tool that will encourage your grandchildren to spend daily time with God? *Our Daily Bread for Kids: 365 Meaningful Moments with God* by Crystal Bowman and Teri McKinley is filled with short stories, easy Bible verses, and applications suited for children ages six to ten.

- Where do you go when you long to sit in God's presence? Is there a place or an activity that nurtures your intimacy with Christ? How can you incorporate more alone time with Jesus in your life? Reflect on James 4:8.

"Whoever keeps his word, in him truly the love of God is perfected. By this we may know that we are in him: whoever says he abides in him ought to walk in the same way in which he walked" (1 John 2:5–6).

"Now, little children, abide in him, so that when he appears we may have confidence and not shrink from him in shame at his coming" (1 John 2:28).

"Jesus said to the Jews who had believed him, 'If you abide in my word, you are truly my disciples'" (John 8:31).

"No one who abides in him keeps on sinning; no one who keeps on sinning has either seen him or known him" (1 John 3:6).

"By this we know that we abide in him and he in us, because he has given us of his Spirit" (1 John 4:13).

"Draw near to God, and he will draw near to you. Cleanse your hands, you sinners, and purify your hearts, you double-minded" (James 4:8).

"If we live by the Spirit, let us also keep in step with the Spirit" (Galatians 5:25).

day thirty

Be Still

We cannot find God in noise or agitation.

Mother Teresa

Be still, and know that I am God.

Psalm 46:10

A glass jar filled with soil and water sits on top of the kitchen cabinets in my friend's house. It is not a new trend in home décor.

She explains the jar is a frequent illustration in her pastor's sermons. She keeps it there as a reminder of an important truth. Sometimes we just need to be still.

When we shake the jar, it quickly becomes a muddy mess. If we let it rest, the dirt eventually settles to the bottom, leaving a clean layer of water on top.

The lesson of the jar: Be still.

Stillness is a struggle for most of us. Our schedules leave little room for such nonactivity. We are in perpetual motion, trying to fix the world.

Mental stillness is even more difficult to achieve. Anxiety and fear stir up our negative thoughts. Worry keeps us awake at night. We fret over the details of our lives. We fret over difficult relationships. We fret over finances. We fret over world affairs.

The dictionary defines *fret* as "to eat or gnaw into."[20] Constant fretting gnaws away at our emotions and physical health.

When the lives of loved ones become messy, we swoop in. We are anything but still. Most of the time, our frenzied, fretful efforts are futile and exhausting. The harder we try, the more our anxious thoughts swirl and confuse us. We jostle the jar, creating a bigger mess.

We need to stop shaking the jar. It is time to let it settle.

Psalm 46:10 gives us a beautiful command from God: "Be still, and know that I am God. I will be exalted among the nations, I will be exalted in the earth!"

Paul Tripp calls Psalm 46 "the ultimate cataclysmic Psalm."[21] Verses 2–3 imagine the earth experiencing a catastrophic event: the earth trembles, the mountains crumble, the oceans foam, and roar. It is terrifying to contemplate such a scene.

Even should that devastation occur, the psalmist declares, "The LORD of hosts is with us; the God of Jacob is our fortress" (v. 11).

Our confidence that God is with us and is our fortress, even when the world is falling apart, brings us comfort.

The "be still" of verse 10 is the result of our "knowing" and believing that the Lord Almighty is sovereign over all life's circumstances. "Be still, and know." Without the knowing, there can be no true stillness.

Our grandchildren are not exempt from anxiety and fear. Mental health professionals report that anxiety and depression in children and adolescents have reached epidemic levels. There are many contributing factors to this rise of distress in our grandchildren. They need our help in learning to calm their anxious thoughts.

In a recent conversation with a counselor friend, she wondered about using a snow globe to help children and adolescents take a moment to still their thoughts. When their worries and anxieties are swirling like snow in a globe, they can silently watch the flakes drift to the bottom. As the snow settles, so do their anxious thoughts; their minds become calm. Sometimes even children need to learn to be still.

Believers have the privilege of being still before the Lord. When our thoughts are swirling, when we are actively fretting, we need to find a quiet place to sit. We need to let our thoughts settle so we can see more clearly. "Be still, and know."

We need to remember that God is in control.

When we read of and meditate on God's love and power, our thoughts begin to settle. Our Father quiets our hearts and minds. We surrender control to Him. We are freed from our fretting. We quit shaking the jar. We model trust in God to our grandchildren.

This is a lesson I need to learn over and over again. Grandparents and grandchildren alike have anxious, fretful thoughts. Grandparents and grandchildren alike need to learn to be still and find true peace. May the Lord give us just the right words to share this truth with our loved ones.

"Be still, and know that I am God" (Psalm 46:10).

Let us pray that . . .

- our grandchildren will learn to be still before God (Psalm 46:10).
- our grandchildren will own the truth and know that God is sovereign (Psalm 46:10).
- our grandchildren will refuse to fret over the unfairness of some of life's problems (Psalm 37:7).
- our grandchildren will learn to wait upon the Lord and trust Him to come to their aid (Psalm 62:5; Isaiah 40:31).
- our grandchildren will find strength in being still before God (Isaiah 30:15).
- our grandchildren will find peace for their anxious thoughts (Philippians 4:6–7).

Heavenly Father, we want to be still. We want peace. We worship you as the Sovereign God over all life's problems. We choose to still ourselves before you and acknowledge you as Lord. We make a muddy mess of things by trying to fix problems that aren't ours to fix. Forgive us for fretting instead of trusting. We pray for our anxious grandchildren. Help them to learn how to sit and settle their thoughts. May we have the opportunity to sit beside them and bring comfort. Help them to turn to your Word for understanding and wisdom. Calm them with your love. Amen.

Think and Do

- Read Isaiah 26:3. Have there been times when your mind was fixed on God? What happened to your swirling thoughts? What were some of the benefits of this kind of mental stillness?
- There is very little "quiet" time for children. *The Silence Slips In* by Alison Hughes treats younger children to the beauty of being still.
- One of my favorite Christmas gifts came from two of my grandsons. Our daughter found a snow globe craft at the local hobby shop. Inside the snow globe she placed a photo of the boys. Perhaps watching the snow settle would help still the swirling thoughts of an anxious grandchild.

"Be still, and know that I am God. I will be exalted among the nations, I will be exalted in the earth!" (Psalm 46:10).

"Be still before the LORD and wait patiently for him; fret not yourself over the one who prospers in his way, over the man who carries out evil devices!" (Psalm 37:7).

"For God alone, O my soul, wait in silence, for my hope is from him" (Psalm 62:5).

"They who wait for the LORD shall renew their strength; they shall mount up with wings like eagles; they shall run and not be weary; they shall walk and not faint" (Isaiah 40:31).

"For thus said the Lord GOD, the Holy One of Israel, 'In returning and rest you shall be saved; in quietness and in trust shall be your strength.'" (Isaiah 30:15).

"Do not be anxious about anything, but in everything by prayer and supplication with thanksgiving let your requests be made known to God. And the peace of God, which surpasses all understanding, will guard your hearts and your minds in Christ Jesus" (Philippians 4:6–7).

day thirty-one

Be Discreet

The true test of a man's spirituality is not his ability to speak, as we are apt to think, but rather his ability to bridle his tongue.

R. Kent Hughes

Discretion will watch over you, understanding will guard you.

Proverbs 2:11

They say confession is good for the soul.

Sharing struggles with a friend keeps us honest and helps us grow. An open conversation with a pastor or mentor steers us in a healthier direction.

For believers, confession brings healing. It is the key that unlocks the door to grace. "If we confess our sins, he is faithful and just to forgive us our sins" (1 John 1:9).

Careful confession is medicine for the soul.

Some sociologists have labeled our society the "confessional society." It is not to a black robed priest or pastor, or even to the Lord himself that some confess their flaws or life's disappointments.

Some confess loudly to the world.

A portion of social media users regularly unload their relational problems, anger, and fears to thousands of "friends" they have never met. Every thought and opinion is seen. Every statement scrutinized and mercilessly bashed by faceless "friends." The commenters rarely have genuine interest in the person's well-being.

Thousands of adolescents report anxiety, depression, and disappointment following online interactions. Their hope for genuine, caring connections clashes with their actual experience. It is incredibly painful.

Young and old, we all need a healthy dose of discretion.

When we are discreet, we use good judgment in choosing what we say. We weigh the benefits of sharing against the potential fallout. We ask ourselves if we are using the best platform to air our thoughts. Can this person (or persons) receive our reflections kindly? Would it be better to hold our tongue or step away from the keyboard?

We use discretion in many areas of life. When preparing for a job interview, we dress discreetly. We avoid flashy outfits that lack seriousness or draw too much attention.

If we are fortunate, after the bills are paid, we have some discretionary income—undesignated income that we can use according to our own common sense. Discretion is critical for a healthy life.

In Proverbs 1:1–4 Solomon stated the theme and purpose of his writings.

> The proverbs of Solomon, son of David, king of Israel:
>
> To know wisdom and instruction,
>   to understand words of insight,
> to receive instruction in wise dealing,
>   in righteousness, justice, and equity;
> to give prudence to the simple,
>   knowledge and *discretion to the youth.* (emphasis added)

Verbal or written discretion is a virtue. It is a product of self-control and wisdom. It shields us from misunderstanding, conflict, and disappointment. Solomon wrote to his son, "Discretion will watch over you, understanding will guard you" (2:11).

Discretion in our speech stops problems before they begin.

Solomon had more to say about discreet speech: "Whoever guards his mouth preserves his life; he who opens wide his lips comes to ruin" (13:3). We have seen the truth of this statement. Good people have been ruined by one moment of indiscreet speech.

"Whoever restrains his words has knowledge, and he who has a cool spirit is a man of understanding" (17:27).

In *Live Not by Lies*, Ron Dreher writes about the struggle for privacy in the former Soviet Union. Soviet authorities went to bizarre lengths to discover the tiniest detail of citizens' lives. The more they knew, the more power they had.

There is a lesson we can learn from the stories he shares of those who suffered from these intrusions. Some information should be openly and joyfully shared. Other life circumstances are so important they deserve to be honored and protected as private.

Our grandchildren need warm, caring, face-to-face relationships where they can learn discretion in real time. I pray each grandchild will come to understand the importance of discretion in speech. May discretion watch over them and keep them safe. May they grow into the confident, loving people we know they can be.

Let us pray that . . .

- our grandchildren will exercise discretion (Proverbs 2:11).
- our grandchildren will restrain their words when appropriate (Proverbs 17:27).
- our grandchildren's speech will be gracious and sweet (Proverbs 16:24).
- our grandchildren will learn to control their speech (James 1:26).
- our grandchildren will grasp the importance of their words (Proverbs 18:21).
- our grandchildren will make "face-to-face" friends rather than relying on many friends from afar (Proverbs 18:24).

Heavenly Father, set a watch over our lips. Keep us from sharing those things which should remain private and keeping private those things that need to be shared. Grant us discretion in our speech. Lord, we pray that our grandchildren will learn discretion. May they exercise discretion in both public and private speech. We pray they will believe that discretion is for their own protection. May their speech be

seasoned with grace and be a blessing to themselves and others. Give them loving, gracious, and safe friends. Amen.

Think and Do

- Interested in reading more about the impact of screen time? *Grandparenting Screen Kids* is a helpful resource. Authors Gary Chapman and Arlene Pellicane remind grandparents that their relationship with grandchildren is more valuable than any electronic device.

- Here are a few questions that might help us with our own social media use. What benefits do I hope to receive from this service? Is social media meeting those goals? How can I set limits?

- Do you know a young person disappointed by comments on social media? Try affirming them that their desire for caring relationships is healthy. Ask them if they think this platform will help them build those kinds of relationships.

"Discretion will watch over you, understanding will guard you" (Proverbs 2:11).

"Whoever restrains his words has knowledge, and he who has a cool spirit is a man of understanding" (Proverbs 17:27).

"Gracious words are like a honeycomb, sweetness to the soul and health to the body" (Proverbs 16:24).

"If anyone thinks he is religious and does not bridle his tongue but deceives his heart, this person's religion is worthless" (James 1:26).

"Death and life are in the power of the tongue, and those who love it will eat its fruits" (Proverbs 18:21).

"A man of many companions may come to ruin, but there is a friend who sticks closer than a brother" (Proverbs 18:24).

day thirty-two

Keep Yourself in God's Love

When you keep the porch light on for the prodigal child, . . . you do what God does every single moment.

Max Lucado

To him who is able to keep you from stumbling and to present you before his glorious presence without fault and with great joy.

Jude v. 24 (NIV)

As often as we can, we avoid the Illinois highways. We prefer the scenic route. Sometimes we just want to take a drive in the country.

As we round a tree-lined curve on one of our favorite side roads, we see a long stretch that leads to Tempel Farms, home to the world-famous Lipizzans. Charming wood-post-and-rail fences provide boundaries for these priceless horses.

Sometimes we see these beautiful animals galloping through the fields. Other times they stand sedately under cozy horse blankets. Smaller fenced-in areas corral the horses when it's time to eat or to be brushed, trained, or exercised.

One thing is always true. At all times, these treasured horses live within the fences. The carefully laid boundaries exist for their protection and allow the owners to provide the expert care the horses need.

The epistle of Jude was written to address the threat of apostasy and heresy. After outlining the dangers that existed both inside and outside the church, Jude encouraged the readers to be intentional in building up and protecting their own precious faith. That was the only way they could protect their vulnerabilities. He encouraged them to stay within the fences.

"Dear friends, by building yourselves up in your most holy faith and praying in the Holy Spirit, keep yourselves in God's love as you wait for the mercy of our Lord Jesus Christ to bring you to eternal life" (Jude vv. 20–21 NIV).

The Living Bible paraphrases verse 21 this way, "Stay always within the boundaries where God's love can reach and bless you."

Jude saw the faith of these believers as precious and in need of care, protection, and constant building up. One commentator wrote that the message of Jude 21 is "stay home." Stay close to the love of God and those relationships and teachings that guard and grow your faith. Stay within the fences.

The prodigal son broke through the fences that kept him in an environment where he could fully experience and benefit from his father's love. Trying to live outside the boundaries of his father's love brought only pain, isolation, abuse, and disgrace. The warmth and fellowship of home was only a stabbing memory.

Hitting rock bottom, hungry, and ashamed, he returned home.

His father was waiting for him. As Max Lucado reminds us, "When you keep the porch light on for the prodigal child, . . . you do what God does every single moment."[22]

Humbled by his experience, grateful to be home, the son now was in a place where his father's love could reach and bless him.

God's carefully laid boundaries exist for our protection and put us in a place where His love can reach and bless us.

It is normal for young people to test the boundaries. Sometimes they wander for a while. Other times they gallop away at frightening speed.

We know God's love can reach them wherever they roam.

I pray that all my grandchildren will keep themselves in the love of God. For those who might wander or even gallop away, I pray that God will put a "hedge of protection" around them. I pray that the prodigal will come home and be welcomed with open arms. I pray that as the years go by, each child will be in a place where they can benefit from the blessings of God's love.

Let us pray that . . .

- our grandchildren will treasure the commands and boundaries laid down by God (Psalm 19:7–11).
- our grandchildren will know that God desires to bless them (Psalm 16:6).
- our grandchildren will avoid friends who will be a negative influence (1 Corinthians 15:33).
- our grandchildren will have friends who will help restore them (James 5:19–20).
- our grandchildren will know that God always forgives (1 John 1:9).
- our grandchildren will know the great love and forgiveness of God (Psalm 103:11–12).
- our grandchildren will know the Father is always waiting (Luke 15:20).

Heavenly Father, we thank you for the boundaries you lay down for our protection. There is no more pleasant place than inside the fences where your love can bless us. Lord, we ask that you open the hearts of our grandchildren to understand the importance of boundaries. When they break through the fences, help us to forgive and restore. We pray you will put a hedge of protection around any who wander far. We know your love can reach them anywhere and at any time. Thank you for your steadfast, unfailing love. Amen.

Think and Do

- *Prayers for Prodigals: 90 Days of Prayer for Your Child* by James Banks can be an encouragement to parents and grandparents in this situation.
- *The Lost Son Comes Home* by Tim Ladwig will make an impression on your grandchildren. Beautifully illustrated and written, this book will touch their hearts as they learn of the Father's love.

- Read and reflect upon Psalm 16. In this emotional psalm, David rejoices in his relationship with God. What blessings did he experience as he stayed close to the Lord?

"The law of the LORD is perfect, reviving the soul; the testimony of the LORD is sure, making wise the simple. . . . More to be desired are they than gold, even much fine gold; sweeter also than honey and drippings of the honeycomb" (Psalm 19:7, 10).

"The lines have fallen for me in pleasant places; indeed, I have a beautiful inheritance" (Psalm 16:6).

"My brothers, if anyone among you wanders from the truth and someone brings him back, let him know that whoever brings back a sinner from his wandering will save his soul from death and will cover a multitude of sins" (James 5:19–20).

"If we confess our sins, he is faithful and just to forgive us our sins and to cleanse us from all unrighteousness" (1 John 1:9).

"For as high as the heavens are above the earth, so great is his steadfast love toward those who fear him; as far as the east is from the west, so far does he remove our transgressions from us" (Psalm 103:11–12).

"He arose and came to his father. But while he was still a long way off, his father saw him and felt compassion, and ran and embraced him and kissed him" (Luke 15:20).

day thirty-three

A Promise and a Plan

God never made a promise that was too good to be true.

D. L. Moody

For all the promises of God find their Yes in him.

2 Corinthians 1:20

"But you promised!"

A guilt-ridden father slumps in a tattered airport chair. He is missing his daughter's first dance recital.

A single mom promises her son a birthday party with friends. Pink slip in hand, her heart breaks as she tells him the party is off.

Nothing upsets a child quite like broken promises. For some, the disappointment lingers. It becomes a fault line in a shaky parent-child relationship.

A promise is sacred to children. It is as binding as a contract drawn up by a lawyer. There is no wiggle room.

Some of this childhood disappointment can be avoided. When we understand the difference between a promise and a plan, we can help our grandchildren manage their disappointment.

Plans are contingent on weather, health, finances, energy, work schedules, and time. A trip to the zoo is a plan. A birthday party is a plan. The purchase of a new game or toy is a plan.

"I will always love you" is a promise.

Plans are made in the hope that all the pieces will fit together. Sometimes they do. Sometimes they don't. Flat tires, illness, snowstorms, doctor bills, and work emergencies are outside of our control.

Plans can change. Plans can be rescheduled.

But not promises. Promises are based on certainty.

"I will always love you." "I will always care for you." "I will always pray for you." These are promises we can keep regardless of weather, finances, or health.

The promises of God are binding. Promises made to His children are given in love.

We can be certain that each of His promises will come to pass. "Not one word of all the good promises that the LORD had made to the house of Israel had failed; all came to pass" (Joshua 21:45).

God is true to His word. God always does what He says He will do. "It is impossible for God to lie" (Hebrews 6:18).

> If we confess our sins, he is faithful and just and will forgive us our sins and purify us from all unrighteousness. (1 John 1:9 NIV)

> Come to me, all who labor and are heavy laden, and I will give you rest. (Matthew 11:28)

> I will never leave you nor forsake you. (Hebrews 13:5)

The Lord is always true to His promises.

God also has a plan. Unlike human plans, external circumstances never derail what God has in mind for His children. Weather, health, finances, and time cannot interfere with God's purposes.

In spite of the loss and pain Job suffered, he continued to be confident that the Sovereign God had a plan. "I know that you can do all things, and that no purpose of yours can be thwarted" (Job 42:2).

We can trust completely in both God's promises and God's plans for our lives. Nothing stops what God desires to do.

Our grandchildren benefit from our promise to love, care, and pray for them. Keeping promises strengthens the bond we share. More importantly, it provides an opportunity to tell them of the Father who both keeps His promises and has a plan for their lives.

I pray my grandchildren will trust in both the promises and plans of God. May they live in the confidence that God's promises are true. They will never be broken.

Let us pray that . . .

- our grandchildren will receive the promise of eternal life (1 John 2:25).

- our grandchildren will believe that God fulfills all His promises (Joshua 21:45).

- our grandchildren will know that Jesus is the fulfillment of all God's promises (2 Corinthians 1:20).

- our grandchildren will be patient as they await the fulfilling of God's promises (2 Peter 3:9).

- our grandchildren will acknowledge God and allow Him to direct their path according to His plan (Proverbs 3:5–6).

- our grandchildren will believe that God has good work for them to do (Ephesians 2:10).

- our grandchildren will believe that no one can thwart God's plan for their lives (Job 42:2).

Heavenly Father, thank you for your precious promises. Everything you promise comes to pass. We are grateful that you have a plan for our lives. We trust you to fulfill it. We want our grandchildren to know your promises and the comfort that they bring. We pray they will seek your plan for their lives. As they trust your promises and plans, may they bring you glory. Amen.

Think and Do

- *The Promises of God Storybook Bible* by Jennifer Lyell uses fifty well-known Bible stories to teach children about God's faithfulness to His promises and plan.

- During my college years, I was given a *Jesus Person Pocket Promise Book*. I can still see the golden sunrise on the cover. How might a return to an emphasis on the promises of God strengthen our children and grandchildren? What promise of God would you like to share with them?
- Do you have a favorite promise from the Bible? Gather up some art supplies and let the artists in your family use their creativity to illustrate the verse.

"This is the promise that he made to us—eternal life" (1 John 2:25).

"Not one word of all the good promises that the LORD had made to the house of Israel had failed; all came to pass" (Joshua 21:45).

"All the promises of God find their Yes in him. That is why it is through him that we utter our Amen to God for his glory" (2 Corinthians 1:20).

"The Lord is not slow to fulfill his promise as some count slowness, but is patient toward you, not wishing that any should perish, but that all should reach repentance" (2 Peter 3:9).

"Trust in the LORD with all your heart, and do not lean on your own understanding. In all your ways acknowledge him, and he will make straight your paths" (Proverbs 3:5–6).

"We are his workmanship, created in Christ Jesus for good works, which God prepared beforehand, that we should walk in them" (Ephesians 2:10).

"I know that you can do all things, and that no purpose of yours can be thwarted" (Job 42:2).

day thirty-four

Sunday Dinner

A world without a Sabbath would be like a man without a smile, like summer without flowers, and like a homestead without a garden. It is the joyous day of the whole week.

Henry Ward Beecher

Remember the Sabbath day, to keep it holy.

Exodus 20:8

The aroma of pot roast escaped from the kitchen. Comics littered the living room floor. Baseball played in the background. A competitive game of checkers with Grandma was followed by a quiet afternoon of reading.

It was Sunday in the 1950s.

Stores were closed on this day of rest. With nowhere to go, we were forced to stay close to home. For twenty-four hours, we did life in slow motion. Even those who didn't attend church knew it was a day set apart to reflect on God. At the very least, the world gave a tip of the hat to that day.

All of society benefited from the quiet rhythms of this day of rest, the Christian Sabbath.

Sunday was my favorite day of the week. It was a day unlike the others. It was quieter, slower, more thoughtful, more relational, more beautiful, and certainly more restful.

Sunday was simply "more" in every way. It was the Lord's Day.

When stores began opening on this precious day of rest, we were surprised and disappointed. Gradually, our shock turned to acceptance. We justified this change. Now, busy moms and dads would have another day to catch up on errands before a new week began.

We wondered, Had our attitudes about the Sabbath been too rigid and legalistic?

Some of us wondered if the competition of commerce and sports would eat away at worship, family time, and rest. My pastor husband suspected it might.

Of all the changes in our culture, this is the one I most often lament. In losing the Sabbath, we have lost so much.

The Sabbath is a beautifully wrapped, carefully chosen gift from our Creator. Yet we stand in line at customer service, ready to exchange it for something that (in the moment) seems more attractive.

We rob ourselves of the worship, beauty, rest, and relational connections the Sabbath promises. We are poorer for it. Echoing Henry Ward Beecher's thoughts, a society that doesn't honor the Sabbath is like "summer without flowers."

Walking through a grain field, Jesus and His disciples picked some heads of grain for food. The Pharisees scolded Jesus for breaking the Sabbath laws.

In response, Jesus corrected their legalistic view of the Sabbath. "The Sabbath was made for man, not man for the Sabbath" (Mark 2:27).

The Sabbath is one of God's gracious gifts to us. When we accept this gift, it restores and renews our souls. In keeping the Sabbath, we declare to the world that we find our rest and peace in God alone.

It is a day unlike all the others. Every day belongs to God, but as someone has said, "The Sabbath is especially His."

The keeping of the Sabbath was an obligation for the Jewish people. It shaped their identity. God's people were known for observing this day of rest. The traditions that surrounded this day—the preparations, the food, the candles, the prayers—influenced their children's understanding of their special relationship with God.

I recently missed an opportunity with my grandchildren. We were gathered around the table to celebrate a two-year-old grandson's birthday with cake and ice cream. Our six-year-old grandson asked, "Grandma, why do you call lunch on Sunday, Sunday dinner? Most people just call it lunch." I don't recall my answer. This is what I wish I had said: "Because Sunday is a day unlike all the others. It is the Lord's Day. It is a gift God has given so we can worship Him, spend more time together as a family, and rest. Because God loves us, He gave us Sunday to add beauty and peace to our lives. What we do on Sunday is different from what we do on all the other days. Even what and when we eat is meant to make the day special and memorable."

Most Sundays, two lonely plates sit side by side on our dining room table. Writing this, I realize I want to change that. I long to fully embrace the beauty of the Sabbath and share this joyous day with the ones I love.

I pray my husband and I will model the meaning of Sabbath to our grandchildren. I pray they will grow in their understanding and allow the gift of the Sabbath to renew and restore them. May they remember the Sabbath day and keep it holy.

Let us pray that . . .

- our grandchildren will carefully and prayerfully consider the role of the fourth commandment in their lives (Exodus 20:8).
- our grandchildren will worship the Lord as part of their Sabbath observance (Psalm 95:6–7).
- our grandchildren will worship the Lord of the Sabbath (Mark 2:28).
- our grandchildren's observance of the Sabbath will not be legalistic but come from a heart of love for God (Colossians 2:16–17).
- our grandchildren will enter the Sabbath rest given to those who believe (Hebrews 4:9).
- our grandchildren will call the Sabbath a delight (Isaiah 58:13–14).

Heavenly Father, we love Sundays. We desperately need rest and relationships, and you have provided a way for us to enjoy both each week. Forgive us for neglecting to keep the Sabbath. Help us to learn

how to honor the day without legalism. Quiet our hearts; calm our spirits. Help us to remember the Sabbath is a day to honor and worship you. We pray that our grandchildren will learn to love Sundays. Quiet their hearts, calm their spirits, turn their hearts to you in worship. We pray they will have joyous days of rest and peace. May they understand the day is a gift from you and for their benefit. We pray that our families will honor the Sabbath and keep it holy. Amen.

Think and Do

- We often use Sundays to prepare for the week. How can you use the week to prepare for Sunday?
- Isaiah 58:13–14 gives an interesting perspective on Sabbath observance. What attitudes were to be encouraged in God's people? How was the Sabbath to be different from the other days of the week for the Israelites?

"Remember the Sabbath day, to keep it holy. Six days you shall labor, and do all your work, but the seventh day is a Sabbath to the LORD your God. On it you shall not do any work, you, or your son, or your daughter, or your male servant, or your female servant, or your livestock, or the sojourner who is within your gates" (Exodus 20:8–10).

"Oh come, let us worship and bow down; let us kneel before the LORD, our Maker! For he is our God, and we are the people of his pasture, and the sheep of his hand" (Psalm 95:6–7).

"The Son of Man is lord even of the Sabbath" (Mark 2:28).

"Therefore let no one pass judgment on you in questions of food and drink, or with regard to a festival or a new moon or a Sabbath. These are a shadow of the things to come, but the substance belongs to Christ" (Colossians 2:16–17).

"There remains a Sabbath rest for the people of God, for whoever has entered God's rest has also rested from his works as God did from his" (Hebrews 4:9–10).

"If you keep your feet from breaking the Sabbath and from doing as you please on my holy day, if you call the Sabbath a delight and the LORD's holy day honorable, and if you honor it by not going your own way and not doing as you please or speaking idle words, then you will find your joy in the LORD, and I will cause you to ride in triumph on the heights of the land and to feast on the inheritance of your father Jacob." For the mouth of the LORD has spoken" (Isaiah 58:13–14 NIV).

day thirty-five

Charity

If I do not give a friend "the benefit of the doubt," but put the worst construction instead of the best on what is said or done, then I know nothing of Calvary love.

Amy Carmichael

Make allowance for each other's faults, and forgive anyone who offends you. Remember, the Lord forgave you, so you must forgive others.

Colossians 3:13 (NLT)

For the most part, we are charitable people.

In 2019, Americans contributed $449.64 billion to charity, making that year one of the highest in charitable-giving history. Personal giving of $309 billion surpassed the donations of foundations and corporations.[23] Volunteers gave millions of hours of service to help their fellow citizens.

These numbers do not reflect the behind-the-scenes sharing of resources by family members, church members, friends, and neighbors. Charitable hearts make a difference.

There is one place where our charity lags behind. At times it is completely absent.

In times of disagreement, we often lack charity. At the very moment a charitable response is needed, we pass judgment on the intents and motives of others.

Authors Greg Lukianoff and Jonathan Haidt share the principle of charity in *The Coddling of the American Mind*.

There is a principle in philosophy and rhetoric called the principle of charity, which says that one should interpret other people's statements in their best, most reasonable form, not in the worst or most offensive way possible.[24]

The principle of charity means we offer others the benefit of the doubt. It allows us to fairly evaluate the opinion of another. It challenges us to look for areas of agreement, no matter how small.

The principle of charity demands we treat even our fiercest opponent with respect. We may demolish a foe's argument, but we must never demolish the person.

We occasionally get a glimpse of this principle on the normally raucous floor of British Parliament. A member rises to challenge a colleague's position. He begins by noting the worthiness of his opponent by addressing him as "my esteemed colleague" or "my worthy opponent." He may even refer to his adversary as "my friend from the other side."

Frequently, the speaker admits to a point of agreement. Then, barely stopping to breathe, he launches into a passionate presentation of his own thoughts and ideas. Fellow ministers pound their desks. The room fills with cheers of "Hear! Hear!" His response may remain charitable throughout. Or it may not.

Mutual respect is critical for effective debate. It is also good manners.

Have your ever been misunderstood? Did you wish you had been given the benefit of the doubt? We always hope others will try to understand our hearts and show generosity.

In the recent past, our grandchildren have witnessed uncharitable and bitter debates. Imagine the change in our homes, churches, neighborhoods, and political scene if we routinely offered others the benefit of the doubt.

Someone must explain the necessity of charity in speech to our grandchildren. All their future relationships will benefit if they learn to offer a charitable response.

Scripture encourages the principle of charity. It admonishes us to be generous even in conversation and conflict.

Make allowance for each other's faults, and forgive anyone who offends you. Remember, the Lord forgave you, so you must forgive others. (Colossians 3:13 NLT)

Good sense makes one slow to anger, and it is his glory to overlook an offense. (Proverbs 19:11)

Whatever you wish that others would do to you, do also to them, for this is the Law and the Prophets. (Matthew 7:12)

Let your speech always be gracious, seasoned with salt, so that you may know how you ought to answer each person. (Colossians 4:6)

Charity does not end with our financial or material gifts. Charity—Christian love—is a guiding principle applicable to every area of life. Even our speech.

I pray my grandchildren will understand the necessity of this principle in all their relationships. May they increasingly show generosity and charity toward others while continuing to hold fast to the truth.

Let us pray that . . .

- our grandchildren will show love even to those with whom they disagree (1 Corinthians 13).
- our grandchildren will be generous and charitable in every area (Luke 6:38).
- our grandchildren's generous words will build others up and not tear them down (Ephesians 4:29).
- our grandchildren will do everything in love (1 Corinthians 16:14).
- our grandchildren will be known as gracious people (Colossians 4:6).
- our grandchildren will show perfect courtesy to others (Titus 3:2).

Heavenly Father, forgive us for being so quick to anger. Forgive us for so easily accusing others of ill motives. Give us the grace to respond charitably, even in disagreement. Help us to offer others the benefit of the doubt. Give us the maturity to overlook slights and small offenses. Enable us to always speak the truth in the most loving way. We pray that our grandchildren will practice charity. Grant them generous and loving spirits that look for the good in others. Help them to have the boldness to speak truth with love. Give them both strength and kindness. We pray their generous, charitable attitudes will be a demonstration of Calvary's love. Amen.

Think and Do

- Think of a situation when someone misunderstood your motives. How did you respond? Could you have responded in a different way that built a better relationship?

- Has there ever been a time when you did not give someone the benefit of the doubt and you wish you had? Have you ever received the benefit of the doubt and a charitable response from someone? How did that change your relationship? Pray that God will give you wisdom to avoid jumping to conclusions about someone's motives. Pray that the Lord will help you to become more charitable in attitude and speech.

- Do any of your grandchildren have an enemy at school? A classmate who might need the benefit of the doubt? *Enemy Pie* by Derek Munson is a fun way to open a conversation about the value of getting to know a person before making a judgment.

"Love is patient and kind; love does not envy or boast; it is not arrogant or rude. It does not insist on its own way; it is not irritable or resentful; it does not rejoice at wrongdoing, but rejoices with the truth. Love bears all things, believes all things, hopes all things, endures all things" (1 Corinthians 13:4–7).

"Give, and it will be given to you. Good measure, pressed down, shaken together, running over, will be put into your lap. For with the measure you use it will be measured back to you" (Luke 6:38).

"Let no corrupting talk come out of your mouths, but only such as is good for building up, as fits the occasion, that it may give grace to those who hear" (Ephesians 4:29).

"Let all that you do be done in love" (1 Corinthians 16:14).

"Let your speech always be gracious, seasoned with salt, so that you may know how you ought to answer each person" (Colossians 4:6).

"To speak evil of no one, to avoid quarreling, to be gentle, and to show perfect courtesy toward all people" (Titus 3:2).

day thirty-six

Harassed and Helpless

After grief for sin there should be joy for forgiveness.

A. W. Pink

As he approached Jerusalem and saw the city, he wept over it.

Luke 19:41 (NIV)

My husband is a Chicago boy. Growing up in a southside suburb, he often hopped a bus to the city to spend Saturdays with friends. He admired the architecture, sauntered down Michigan Avenue, took the elevator to the top of the Prudential Building (the tallest building in the windy city at that time), and grabbed a burger before heading home.

His mother never gave a second thought to his safety. It was the early 1960s.

We love the city. Our kids love the city. In the past, we spent hours wandering through the art museum or eating lunch at a restaurant near Navy Pier. Caramel corn from Garrett Popcorn Shop was our favorite snack for the drive home.

Downtown Chicago is only an hour's drive from our home. But we haven't gone in years. The city has changed.

A documentary aired on cable TV addressed the violence that has gripped the city. Hours of disturbing film revealed the depth of the crisis. Shootings, muggings, stabbings, carjackings, and looting are crimes mostly perpetrated by young adults.

As the program ended, I saw the sadness on my husband's face.

Two words came immediately to mind: *harassed* and *helpless*.

Jesus went from town to town, village to village, healing the sick and preaching the good news. Matthew 9 reveals the heart of Jesus as He walked those dusty roads: "When he saw the crowds, he had compassion for them, because they were harassed and helpless, like sheep without a shepherd" (v. 36).

In another instance, Jesus mourned over the city of Jerusalem. "When he drew near and saw the city, he wept over it, saying, 'Would that you, even you, had known on this day the things that make for peace! But now they are hidden from your eyes'" (Luke 19:41–42).

Jesus wept. He wept for the city. He wept over their lack of faith. He wept over their blindness. He wept over their rejection of His offer of true peace. God had a unique plan for the city of Jerusalem, but the people refused it.

Jesus didn't just shed a quiet tear. The Greek word for *wept* means "intense sobbing."[25] Some translations say He "wept aloud."

In Chicago, a city of three million, there are pockets of violence and despair. Thousands of hardworking citizens are harassed and helpless. Children live in difficult situations caused by poverty and other social issues. Instead of playing with friends, enjoying school, preparing for a bright future, they are carrying high levels of stress that could have a lifelong impact.

Would Jesus walk down the Magnificent Mile and weep for Chicago? Would He weep aloud for New York City, Los Angeles, St. Louis, San Francisco, Mexico City, Paris, London, Berlin, Tokyo, Delhi, Johannesburg, and every town large or small?

Moms and dads, grandmas and grandpas worry about their children and grandchildren who live too close to the violence. They feel helpless to improve these troubling situations. Only Jesus can bring lasting peace to our cities.

We weep for Chicago and all our large cities. We realize we need to pray for the millions of good citizens who desire peace. We need to pray especially for the children who call these cities home. Let us also pray for the heartbroken parents and grandparents of children who live in high crime areas. They need our emotional and prayerful support.

Let us pray that . . .

- God will revive our cities, towns, and villages again (Psalm 85:6).
- we will be faithful in prayer for the peace and prosperity of our cities (Jeremiah 29:7).
- we will be earnest in our prayers, remembering that they are powerful (James 5:16).
- God will restore and shine His face upon our cities, children, and grandchildren (Psalm 80:19).
- God will strengthen the hearts of parents and grandparents as they faithfully pray (Psalm 119:28; 1 Chronicles 16:11).
- brokenhearted parents and grandparents will be confident that God is near (Psalm 34:18).
- we will not turn a blind eye to the needs of the hurting in our communities but will show the compassion of Jesus (1 John 3:17–18).
- God will send laborers into these fields (Matthew 9:37–38).

Heavenly Father, we know you love and care for people who are harassed and helpless wherever they live. Bind up and soothe the wounds that cause such pain. We pray for the children who live with the anxiety caused by living in high crime areas. Grant them peace. Convict their elected officials of the need to make the safety of children a top priority. Our hearts ache for the thousands who are harassed by addiction. May the love of Jesus heal their wounded souls and bring hope to their families. We pray for those loving grandparents who fear for the future of their grandchildren. Give them courage, strength, and peace. Turn their sorrow into rejoicing. Amen.

Think and Do

- Pray for your own city. *Seek God for the City*, published by Way-Makers, is a useful guide.

- If you are a grandmother carrying a heavy load of concern, know that others are praying for you. Find a group of kindred spirits to pray along with you.
- Read and meditate on Psalm 82:3–4. Are you aware of any ministries at work in your city? What can you contribute that will help them to fulfill the commands in this psalm?

"Will you not revive us again, that your people may rejoice in you? Show us your steadfast love, O LORD, and grant us your salvation" (Psalm 85:6).

"Seek the welfare of the city where I have sent you into exile, and pray to the LORD on its behalf, for in its welfare you will find your welfare" (Jeremiah 29:7).

"Therefore, confess your sins to one another and pray for one another, that you may be healed. The prayer of a righteous person has great power as it is working" (James 5:16).

"Restore us, O LORD God of hosts! Let your face shine, that we may be saved!" (Psalm 80:19).

"My soul melts away for sorrow; strengthen me according to your word!" (Psalm 119:28).

"Seek the LORD and his strength; seek his presence continually!" (1 Chronicles 16:11).

"The LORD is near to the brokenhearted and saves the crushed in spirit. Many are the afflictions of the righteous, but the LORD delivers him out of them all" (Psalm 34:18–19).

"If anyone has the world's goods and sees his brother in need, yet closes his heart against him, how does God's love abide in him? Little children, let us not love in word or talk but in deed and in truth" (1 John 3:17–18).

"When he saw the crowds, he had compassion for them, because they were harassed and helpless, like sheep without a shepherd. Then he said to his disciples, 'The harvest is plentiful, but the laborers are few; therefore pray earnestly to the Lord of the harvest to send out laborers into his harvest'" (Matthew 9:36–38).

day thirty-seven

Hold Fast

Faith . . . is the art of holding on to things your reason has once accepted, in spite of your changing moods.

C. S. Lewis

I cling to you; your right hand upholds me.

Psalm 63:8 (NIV)

She was only twenty-five. While other young women were establishing careers, dreaming of weddings, or planning adventures, Kayla Mueller laced up her shoes and walked down an unconventional and risky path.

The Christian compassion modeled by her church and parents fueled her concern for the suffering people of the world. It was no surprise when she abandoned the comfort and safety of home for one of the most dangerous places on earth.

In 2013, Kayla began working in Syria with Doctors Without Borders. One August day, as she left a hospital in Aleppo, Kayla was kidnapped by ruthless ISIS soldiers. For months, she survived in the most distressing conditions. Although she was being held with other foreign captives, she was singled out for the harshest treatment.

Her fellow hostages recall the day one of her captors paraded her in front of them. A fellow terrorist taunted her and boasted that Kayla had converted to Islam. Her friends recalled her fearlessly responding, "No, I didn't!"[26]

In 2015, ISIS announced that Kayla had died in captivity.

During her imprisonment, Kayla secretly wrote letters to her parents. Her words reveal not only her bravery but her determination to hold fast to her faith.

> I remember mom always telling me that all in all in the end the only one you really have is God. I have come to a place in experience where, in every sense of the word, I have surrendered myself to our creator b/c literally there was no one else.[27]

In Revelation 2:13, the apostle John wrote to the church in Pergamum: "I know where you dwell, where Satan's throne is. Yet you hold fast my name." In the worst place, in the worst of circumstances, Kayla Mueller held fast to God's name.

Repeatedly, Scripture urges us to hold fast.

As God's people traveled to their new home, Moses urged them to hold fast to God. "Fear the LORD your God and serve him. Hold fast to him" (Deuteronomy 10:20 NIV). The Hebrew phrase for *hold fast* can also mean to "glue" oneself to another.

The psalmist, during a time of distress, described holding fast to God in this way: "I cling to you; your right hand upholds me" (Psalm 63:8 NIV). David intentionally glued himself to God. Holding fast to God, the psalmist made a remarkable discovery. God was holding on to him.

Paul wrote of holding fast. His encouragement to the people of Philippi included "holding fast to the word of life" (Philippians 2:16).

The writer of Hebrews, reminding the believers they had a great high priest in heavenly places, encouraged these believers to "hold firmly to the faith we profess" (Hebrews 4:14 NIV).

Throughout Christian history, saints have held fast to their faith. For some, holding fast cost them their lives. For others, holding fast strengthened their witness and triggered revival. Even today, Christians around the world continue to hold fast in spite of persecution.

Kayla Mueller, her very life threatened, surrounded by irrational hatred, separated from the people she loved, found it within herself (with God's help) to hold fast to her faith. We can be confident that God was with her, holding her fast.

Let us pray that in days of trouble or of ease, God will enable us to hold fast to His name, His word, and our faith. Let us pray that our grandchildren will cling to, glue themselves to, and hold fast to God.

Let us pray that . . .

- our grandchildren will hold fast to God and never loosen their grip (Deuteronomy 10:20).
- our grandchildren will cling to God (Psalm 63:8).
- our grandchildren will hold fast to the Word of God as the source of truth (Philippians 2:14–16; Titus 1:9; Hebrews 4:14).
- our grandchildren will hold fast to the hope they have in Jesus (Hebrews 10:23).
- our grandchildren will hold fast to what is good, no matter what the world says (1 Thessalonians 5:21; Colossians 2:8).
- our grandchildren will be steadfast to the end (Hebrews 3:14; Revelation 3:11).
- persecuted Christians are able to hold fast to their faith (Hebrews 13:3).

Father, in times of trouble, when we are weak, we sometimes loosen our grip. In those moments, help us to hold fast to what we believe. We choose to cling to you for our support and strength. We pray that our grandchildren will learn to cling to you in the difficulties of life. Strengthen their grip. Help them to hold fast in every situation. When many around them are wavering, their lights flickering, grant our grandchildren a sure and strong faith. Give them the resolve of David, Daniel, and Esther, who held fast to you. Amen.

Think and Do

- Children love heroes. The Bible is filled with stories of men and women who bravely held fast to God. Glenn Hascall's *My Big Book of Bible Heroes Devotional* may be a great addition to your library.

- Have you ever had a toddler cling to you? Have you seen a vine embedded in a tree by years of clinging? In Psalm 63, David rejoices over his relationship with the Lord. In verse 8, he declares his intent to cling to God. Consider the ways you can tighten your grip and cling to the Lord.

"Fear the LORD your God and serve him. Hold fast to him and take your oaths in his name" (Deuteronomy 10:20 NIV).

"My soul clings to you; your right hand upholds me" (Psalm 63:8).

"Do all things without grumbling or disputing, that you may be blameless and innocent, children of God without blemish in the midst of a crooked and twisted generation, among whom you shine as lights in the world, holding fast to the word of life, so that in the day of Christ I may be proud that I did not run in vain or labor in vain" (Philippians 2:14–16).

"He must hold firm to the trustworthy word as taught, so that he may be able to give instruction in sound doctrine and also to rebuke those who contradict it" (Titus 1:9).

"Therefore, since we have a great high priest who has ascended into heaven, Jesus the Son of God, let us hold firmly to the faith we profess" (Hebrews 4:14 NIV).

"Let us hold fast the confession of our hope without wavering, for he who promised is faithful" (Hebrews 10:23).

"Test everything; hold fast what is good" (1 Thessalonians 5:21).

"See to it that no one takes you captive by philosophy and empty deceit, according to human tradition, according to the elemental spirits of the world, and not according to Christ" (Colossians 2:8).

"For we have come to share in Christ, if indeed we hold our original confidence firm to the end" (Hebrews 3:14).

"I am coming soon. Hold fast what you have, so that no one may seize your crown" (Revelation 3:11).

"Remember those who are in prison, as though in prison with them, and those who are mistreated, since you also are in the body" (Hebrews 13:3).

day thirty-eight

The Pickle Barrel

Never be afraid to trust an unknown future to a known God.

Corrie ten Boom

The eternal God is your dwelling place, and underneath are the everlasting arms.

Deuteronomy 33:27

It was 1901. Annie Edson Taylor was desperate.

Annie came from an affluent home. Her parents provided her with everything she could ever want or need. While attending teacher training school, Annie met and fell in love with David Taylor. The young couple married and soon had a baby boy. He died within days of his birth.

Unbelievably, tragedy struck the young wife a second time. David lost his life in the Civil War. All alone, grieving two devastating losses, Annie took her teaching skills on the road. This vagabond life left her with no home and very little money. Annie feared her golden years would be riddled with poverty.

Fascinated by newspaper stories of barrels plummeting over Niagara Falls, she concocted a bizarre retirement plan. She would be the first person (and woman) to go over the falls in a barrel. People would pay to see that!

Annie outfitted the inside of a pickle barrel with pillows, straps, and a small anvil. On October 24, 1901—her sixty-third birthday—Annie and her pickle barrel tumbled wildly over the falls.

When the bobbing barrel came to rest on a rock, Annie emerged unscathed but dazed. Her adventure earned her the title "Queen of the Mist." But it earned her little else.

The moral of the story: Don't trust your future to a pickle barrel.

For centuries, retirees had little savings, no retirement plans, no 401(k)s. We can understand Annie's desperation.

Financial insecurity creates distress. Young adults financing college or launching into the adult world, newly marrieds hoping to purchase a home, families dealing with doctor bills, or seniors transitioning to retirement—all face uncertainty.

Like Annie, they wonder what the future holds for them.

Unlike Annie, they don't need to trust their future to a pickle barrel.

We can trust our future to God. We can trust Him because He sees and He cares.

Jesus reassures us of His care in verses we have loved since childhood. "Are not two sparrows sold for a penny? Yet not one of them will fall to the ground outside your Father's care. And even the very hairs of your head are all numbered. So don't be afraid; you are worth more than many sparrows" (Matthew 10:29–31 NIV).

We are worth more than many sparrows. God will tenderly care for us.

Spring and summer, tiny birds perch on the window boxes outside my bedroom. Each time I see them hopping by, I am reminded how attentively God cares for even the tiniest in His creation. How much more He cares for me.

In the Sermon on the Mount, Jesus commands us to set our anxiety aside and put our faith in His care.

Which of you by being anxious can add a single hour to his span of life? And why are you anxious about clothing? Consider the lilies of the field, how they grow: they neither toil nor spin, yet I tell you, even Solomon in all his glory was not arrayed like one of these. But if God so clothes the grass of the field, which today is alive and tomorrow is thrown into the oven, will he not much more clothe you, O you of little faith? (Matthew 6:27–30)

God intimately cares for every part of His creation. We are no exception. We can trust Him to provide for us. We can trade anxiety for faith.

Each of our grandchildren will be faced with multiple bouts of insecurity. Whether their uncertainty is related to finances, relationships, work, or health, they will be tempted to fret and worry. They may feel as if they are tumbling over the falls in a barrel.

At those times, may they remember God's tender care for the sparrow and rejoice in the splendor of the lilies of the fields.

They can trust their future to the God who sees and cares for them.

Let us pray that . . .

- our grandchildren will trust in God's daily care (Matthew 6:11).

- our grandchildren will remember that God values them and cares for them (Matthew 10:29–31).

- our grandchildren will trust their life's path to the Lord (Proverbs 3:5–6).

- our grandchildren will trust the Lord to meet their needs (Philippians 4:19).

- our grandchildren will make seeking the Lord their priority and trust God to give them what they need (Matthew 6:33).

- our grandchildren will cast all their cares and anxieties about the future upon the Lord (1 Peter 5:7).

- our grandchildren will turn to God for wisdom as they plan for the future (James 1:5).

Heavenly Father, we are amazed that you know and care for the tiniest part of creation. You know and understand the tiniest detail of our lives. We pray our grandchildren will turn to you in the uncertainties of life. We pray that they will look to you in faith in their times of need. Help them to learn the lesson of the sparrow. Help them to regard the lilies of the field. When life feels as if it is tumbling out

of control, may each precious child learn to rest confidently in your everlasting arms. Amen.

Think and Do

- Max Lucado's *The Boy and the Ocean* is the story of a boy and his parents discovering the greatness of God's love as they explore God's creation.

- In response to God's help in battle, Samuel set up a stone and named it Ebenezer—the stone of help. "Thus far the LORD has helped us" (1 Samuel 7:12 NIV). The Ebenezer reminded Samuel and everyone who passed that way of God's faithfulness and care for Israel. How has the Lord cared for you? How can you remember His generosity and share it with your grandchildren? I have a friend who gives newlyweds the gift of an Ebenezer vase with a bag of rocks and a permanent marker. She knows that keeping record of God's specific help glorifies Him, reminds us of His care, and strengthens our faith for the future.

"Give us this day our daily bread" (Matthew 6:11).

"Are not two sparrows sold for a penny? And not one of them will fall to the ground apart from your Father. But even the hairs of your head are all numbered. Fear not, therefore; you are of more value than many sparrows" (Matthew 10:29–31).

"Trust in the LORD with all your heart, and do not lean on your own understanding. In all your ways acknowledge him, and he will make straight your paths" (Proverbs 3:5–6).

"My God will supply every need of yours according to his riches in glory in Christ Jesus" (Philippians 4:19).

"Seek first the kingdom of God and his righteousness, and all these things will be added to you" (Matthew 6:33).

"Humble yourselves, therefore, under the mighty hand of God so that at the proper time he may exalt you, casting all your anxieties on him, because he cares for you" (1 Peter 5:6–7).

"If any of you lacks wisdom, let him ask God, who gives generously to all without reproach, and it will be given him" (James 1:5).

day thirty-nine

Heart and Soul

God will look to every soul like its first love because He is its first love.

C. S. Lewis

Love the Lord your God with all your heart and with all your soul and with all your mind.

Matthew 22:37

In our childhood home, playing "Heart and Soul" was a favorite after-school activity. Susan played the left hand, while Lisa or I thumped out the melody on a battered black piano. Together, we sang our own fractured version of that familiar song.

Heart and soul
I fell in love with you, heart and soul.
I fell in love with you madly.
I fell in love with you. I fell in love with you.

On February 23, 1968, I fell madly in love with Jesus—heart and soul. Whenever I hear that tune, I have flashbacks of those first days of loving Jesus with all my heart.

After months of searching my Bible and talking with Christian friends, it was clear. God was calling me. He had given His life for me. Now the time had come for me to give my life to Him—completely.

I had no idea of the ways that decision would change the trajectory of my life. The Bible came alive. Obedience became both a goal and a

183

desire. Suddenly, church was a place where I was comfortable. People of every age and background became my Christian family.

I looked for any opportunity to spend time with Christian friends. Shy as I was, I enjoyed telling others about God's love. What else could I do? Jesus had washed my sins away and the weight of guilt was gone.

I had a future. In the well-worn phrase of that day, I was certain that God loved me and had a wonderful plan for my life.

In Revelation 2:3–5 the church in Ephesus received a grave warning:

> I know you are enduring patiently and bearing up for my name's sake, and you have not grown weary. But I have this against you, that you have abandoned the love you had at first. Remember therefore from where you have fallen; repent, and do the works you did at first.

This church was in danger. They had abandoned their first love. They had stopped doing the things that elevated Christ to first place in their affections and ministries. What could be worse than losing your first love?

Loving God above all else is a consistent theme of Scripture. We find commands to love God with all our heart and soul in both the Old and New Testaments.

"Hear, O Israel: The LORD our God, the LORD is one. Love the LORD your God with all your heart and with all your soul and with all your strength" (Deuteronomy 6:4–5 NIV).

Love God with all your heart and soul.

When Jesus was asked the question, "Which is the great commandment?" He answered, "You shall love the Lord your God with all your heart and with all your soul and with all your mind. This is the great and first commandment" (Matthew 22:36–38).

Loving God with all our heart and soul is a defining characteristic of the Christian life.

It is easy to maintain our first love in the early days. It is as if we have come to life—because we have.

The world is filled with wonder. We have an unexplainable energy. We feel and understand things we never did before. Knowing more of Jesus is our priority and passion.

As the years go by, our love cools. It happens so gradually we barely notice. Some would describe this process as a slow fade. Like the Ephesians, we may be enduring and bearing up patiently. But through neglect, distraction, and unconfessed sin, our relationship with Christ has faded. It is not what it once was. The joy is gone.

Revelation 2:5 prescribes the remedy for this condition. "Remember therefore from where you have fallen; repent, and do the works you did at first."

Remember. Repent. Return.

Remember those early days of our relationship with Christ. Remember being in awe of His sacrificial love. Remember the freedom. Remember the fellowship of believers, the power of the Word, the joy of obedience.

Repent of our neglect and apathy. Repent of allowing success, other relationships, material possessions to distract us. Repent of unconfessed sin. Repent of allowing our love to grow cold.

Return to the things we once did. Return to meditating upon God's love. Return to Bible study, small groups, personal confession, and prayer. Return to sharing our faith, seeking the lost, meeting needs, encouraging the discouraged. Return to the fellowship of believers. Return to Jesus as the Lord of our lives.

The world needs Christians who love Jesus with all their hearts and souls. People with a fresh love for Jesus are the most effective evangelists of all.

I pray that each of my grandchildren will experience those glorious first days of loving Jesus with all their heart and all their soul. I also pray that they will do those things that will let their love for Jesus burn hotter with every passing year.

Let us pray that . . .

- our grandchildren will love God with all their beings (Mark 12:30–31).

- our grandchildren will understand that God loved them first (1 John 4:19; Romans 5:8).

- our grandchildren's hearts will be directed to the love of God (2 Thessalonians 3:5).
- our grandchildren will abide in God's love and be filled with joy (John 15:10).
- our grandchildren will love their brothers and sisters in Christ (John 13:34).
- our grandchildren will express love for God through obedience (John 14:15).
- our grandchildren's love will not grow cold because of sin (Matthew 24:12).
- our grandchildren will guard their first love (Revelation 2:4–5).

Heavenly Father, thank you for those amazing days of first love for Jesus. We saw your love and goodness everywhere. You were real. How we would love to recover that joy, peace, and purpose. We repent of neglecting our love relationship with you. We repent of allowing other things to replace our time alone with you. We return to doing those things that cultivate a deeper love. May our grandchildren love Jesus with all their hearts and all their souls. Help them to do all that is needed to keep their love fresh and alive. May their fervor and zeal draw others to Christ. Jesus, you are our first love. Amen.

Think and Do

- Do you remember your days of first love for Jesus? Take a few moments to journal about that time. How do you feel about those memories? How can you return to the days of your first love?
- Have you ever written out your testimony? At www.cru.org you can find resources for preparing a written testimony. Remembering who we were before Christ and where He has taken us can rekindle our first love.

"You shall love the Lord your God with all your heart and with all your soul and with all your mind and with all your strength" (Mark 12:30).

"We love because he first loved us" (1 John 4:19).

"For one will scarcely die for a righteous person—though perhaps for a good person one would dare even to die—but God shows his love for us in that while we were still sinners, Christ died for us" (Romans 5:7–8).

"May the Lord direct your hearts to the love of God and to the steadfastness of Christ" (2 Thessalonians 3:5).

"If you keep my commandments, you will abide in my love, just as I have kept my Father's commandments and abide in his love" (John 15:10).

"A new commandment I give to you, that you love one another: just as I have loved you, you also are to love one another" (John 13:34).

"If you love me, you will keep my commandments" (John 14:15).

"Because lawlessness will be increased, the love of many will grow cold" (Matthew 24:12).

"I have this against you, that you have abandoned the love you had at first. Remember therefore from where you have fallen; repent, and do the works you did at first. If not, I will come to you and remove your lampstand from its place, unless you repent" (Revelation 2:4–5).

day forty

On Bended Knee

A day must come in our lives, as definite as the day of our conversion, when we give up all right to ourselves and submit to the absolute lordship of Jesus Christ.

Watchman Nee

Oh come, let us worship and bow down; let us kneel before the LORD, our Maker!

Psalm 95:6

A hopelessly romantic groom-to-be dropped to one knee in a crowded baseball stadium. With the smell of popcorn and hot dogs floating by, he held out a diamond to the love of his life. The surprising proposal was splashed across the jumbotron to the cheers of the crowd.

She said, "Yes!"

Where did this tradition of proposing on bended knee begin? In medieval times, men received their knighthood by kneeling before their king. The gesture showed humility and allegiance. On one knee, with head bowed, the knight repeated an oath pledging his faithfulness and loyalty. Very much like wedding vows.

Eventually, this practice made its way into the world of romance.

Kneeling is also found in the Bible, but it has deeper meaning than knighthood or a marriage proposal. It signifies absolute dependence. It is a sign of humility and loyalty to God. It embodies surrender.

Daniel knelt in prayer three times a day. Jesus knelt in prayer in Gethsemane. Paul told the Ephesian believers that on their behalf he knelt in prayer before the Father. Kneeling is often associated with supplication. In the New Testament, the needy often fell to their knees, crying out for the help of Jesus.

Psalm 95:6 invites us to kneel in worship before our Maker. "Oh come, let us worship and bow down; let us kneel before the Lord, our Maker!"

Kneeling and worship go hand in hand. We love to imagine the adoring shepherds kneeling at the straw-filled manger. The disciples knelt in worship at the Transfiguration. The book of Revelation mentions kneeling over twenty times, as the elders and multitudes kneel to worship the Lamb of God.

Mordecai refused to kneel in subservience to wicked Haman (Esther 3:2). Such kneeling would have indicated his allegiance to Haman and his authority.

In Philippians 2:10–11, Paul says, "At the name of Jesus every knee should bow, in heaven and on earth and under the earth, and every tongue confess that Jesus Christ is Lord, to the glory of God the Father." The word *bow* means "to bend . . . the knee."[28] Bending the knee was exactly what Haman wanted from Mordecai. Bending the knee means giving up one's rights. To bend the knee is to honor and submit oneself entirely to the lordship of another.

Bending the knee for the Christian is an acknowledgment that all we have comes from God. He is our strength. He is our Sovereign. He is our King. He is worthy of all honor. It is to Him alone that we bend the knee.

One day every knee shall bow before Jesus. Every person who has ever lived will kneel and confess Jesus Christ as Lord. All will bend the knee in acknowledgment of His authority.

I pray that our grandchildren will humbly kneel in worship and prayer. I pray they will not hesitate to fall to their knees and cry out for the help of Jesus. I pray they will bend the knee in surrender.

During their time on earth, may each "bend the knee" to Jesus and honor Him alone as their Lord.

Let us pray that . . .

- our grandchildren will kneel in worship to God alone (Luke 4:8).
- our grandchildren will kneel at God's footstool (recognizing His high and exalted position and preeminence over all creation) and worship Him (Psalm 99:5).

- our grandchildren will kneel before God in prayer during times of need (Matthew 15:25; 17:14–15).

- our grandchildren will kneel in worship and recognition of Jesus as the Son of God (Matthew 16:16).

- our grandchildren will bend the knee and submit to God's will as Jesus did in the garden (Luke 22:41–42).

- our grandchildren will kneel before Christ and acknowledge Him as Lord (Philippians 2:9–11).

Heavenly Father, we humbly kneel in worship. We expectantly kneel in prayer. We willingly bend the knee in submission to you as our Lord and Savior. Cleanse our hearts from the pride that keeps us from surrender. We pray, Lord, that our grandchildren will kneel before you. Like the shepherds at the manger, may they kneel in worship of Christ. May they surrender and acknowledge the absolute lordship of Jesus. Amen.

Think and Do

- Take a few minutes to "bow down and worship" the Lord. Meditate on these aspects of God's nature: Almighty, Beautiful, Comforter, Creator, Delight, Deliverer, Eternal One, Everlasting Father, Faithful One, Forgiver, Friend, Generous, Good, Gracious, Healer, Holy, Hope, Inexhaustible, Infinite, Just, Kind, King, Lamb of God, Light of the World, Loving, Merciful, Mighty, Never Changing, Omnipotent, Omnipresent, Omniscient, Peace, Powerful, Present, Quietness, Redeemer, Righteousness, Rock, Savior, Shepherd, Song, Strength, Triumphant, Trustworthy, Truth, Unfailing, Victorious, Wonderful, Worthy of Praise.

- You may want to teach your grandchildren the ABCs of God's nature. Tiny Theologians offers ABC flash cards for God's attributes as well as for the names of God: www.tinytheologians.shop.

"Jesus answered him, 'It is written "You shall worship the Lord your God, and him only shall you serve"'" (Luke 4:8).

"Exalt the LORD our God; worship at his footstool! Holy is he!" (Psalm 99:5).

"A Canaanite woman from that region came out and was crying, 'Have mercy on me, O Lord, Son of David; my daughter is severely oppressed by a demon.' But he did not answer her a word. And his disciples came and begged him, saying, 'Send her away, for she is crying out after us.' He answered, 'I was sent only to the lost sheep of the house of Israel.' But she came and knelt before him, saying, 'Lord, help me'" (Matthew 15:22–25).

"When they came to the crowd, a man came up to him and, kneeling before him, said, 'Lord, have mercy on my son, for he has seizures and he suffers terribly'" (Matthew 17:14–15).

"He said to them, 'But who do you say that I am?' Simon Peter replied, 'You are the Christ, the Son of the living God'" (Matthew 16:15–16).

"He withdrew from them about a stone's throw, and knelt down and prayed, saying, 'Father, if you are willing, remove this cup from me. Nevertheless, not my will, but yours, be done'" (Luke 22:41–42).

"God has highly exalted him and bestowed on him the name that is above every name, so that at the name of Jesus every knee should bow, in heaven and on earth and under the earth, and every tongue confess that Jesus Christ is Lord, to the glory of God the Father" (Philippians 2:9–11).

day forty-one

Discernment

Discernment is not a matter of simply telling the difference between right and wrong; rather it is telling the difference between right and almost right.

Charles Spurgeon

People without discernment are doomed.

Hosea 4:14 (HCSB)

Dad spent hours roaming flea markets and antique malls. A collector of rare books, he was on a never-ending search for more inventory, especially volumes on American history. He loved the five-dollar boxes of books tucked away in the back of stores. Books that owners deemed worthless sat forgotten in broken-down boxes and were sold for next to nothing.

My father rifled nonchalantly through box after box. When he saw a book he suspected was of value, he rarely reacted. Handing his cash to the seller, he shook his head and muttered, "Probably nothing good in here." We knew better.

My father could tell a good book from a bad book. He could discern a valuable book from a worthless one. His years of reading and studying had given him a depth of knowledge few others had. When it came to antique books, my dad had discernment.

Discernment is not a word we often hear. It is an ability we use even less.

Discernment is the ability to recognize or perceive the differences between things. When we exercise discernment, we pause and carefully consider an issue. We thoughtfully evaluate, weigh, and compare. We take time to reflect on the impact of choosing one thing over another.

For the Christian, discernment carries a spiritual dimension. Our ability to exercise discernment comes from knowing God's Word, the Spirit at work in our lives, and prayer. Discernment is a gift as well as a necessity for believers.

In 1 Kings 3:9, Solomon prayed that God would give him "an understanding mind to govern your people, that I may discern between good and evil." Christians who cultivate a discerning mind easily distinguish between good and evil, right and wrong, better and best. They can differentiate between what is of God and what is of man.

Spiritual discernment is critical to understanding God's will. "Do not be conformed to this world, but be transformed by the renewal of your mind, that by testing you may discern what is the will of God, what is good and acceptable and perfect" (Romans 12:2).

Discernment helps us to detect what is false and embrace what is true. "Beloved, do not believe every spirit, but test the spirits to see whether they are from God, for many false prophets have gone out into the world" (1 John 4:1).

Discernment has been replaced with emotional reasoning. Feelings have become the primary tool in decision-making. Young people are bombarded with the message, "Follow your heart." Jeremiah 17:9 tells us that the heart is not to be trusted. "The heart is deceitful above all things, and desperately sick; who can understand it?"

More often than not, decisions made solely on feelings are costly and bring disaster. But true discernment protects and guides. It helps us know what is right and what is wrong, what is true and what is false, what is better and what is best.

Place two books in front of my father and he would quickly discern which book was worth an investment and which was not. His discernment came from years of study and experience.

I imagine sending my grandchildren out into the world with a spiritual and emotional toolbox. When they are faced with a dilemma and turn to the toolbox for help, I hope the first tool they reach for is discernment.

Given the challenges they face, I am praying daily for their discernment. I pray they will be able to tell what is good from what is bad, what is worthless from what is valuable, what is better from what is best.

May they, through study, prayer, and life experiences, become people of great discernment.

Let us pray that . . .

- our grandchildren will be able to discern between truth and falsehood (1 John 4:1).
- our grandchildren will be given an understanding mind to discern between good and evil (1 Kings 3:9).
- our grandchildren will never confuse evil for good (Isaiah 5:20).
- our grandchildren will be transformed by God's Word and will discern His perfect will (Romans 12:2).
- our grandchildren will exercise discernment regarding their own spiritual lives (1 Corinthians 11:31).
- our grandchildren will abound in discernment and have hearts that love the good (Philippians 1:9–10).

Heavenly Father, we pray as Solomon did for hearts that can discern good from evil and right from wrong. Renew our minds with your Word so we can discern your will. May our grandchildren develop hearts and minds that can discern right from wrong and truth from falsehood. Open their eyes to clearly see the difference between good and evil. Grant them good judgment in their friendships and romantic relationships. Give them a love for your Word that will enable them to become discerning. Surround them with godly, discerning people who can encourage them. We pray that from our grandchildren's generation you will raise up an army of discerning believers. Amen.

Think and Do

- Pray for discernment for our spiritual and governmental leaders. Pray for families to be led by discerning parents.

- We all need greater discernment in daily life. Where would you like to become more discerning? In relationships? Finances? Grandparenting? Ask the Lord for wisdom and greater discernment.

- Romans 12:2 gives believers a prescription for growing in discernment. It begins with a transformation in thinking. What can you learn from this verse that will help you to grow in discernment? What steps will you take? What will be the outcome of this transformation?

"Beloved, do not believe every spirit, but test the spirits to see whether they are from God, for many false prophets have gone out into the world" (1 John 4:1).

"Give your servant therefore an understanding mind to govern your people, that I may discern between good and evil, for who is able to govern this your great people?" (1 Kings 3:9).

"Woe to those who call evil good and good evil" (Isaiah 5:20).

"Do not be conformed to this world, but be transformed by the renewal of your mind, that by testing you may discern what is the will of God, what is good and acceptable and perfect" (Romans 12:2).

"For if we discerned ourselves, we wouldn't be judged" (1 Corinthians 11:31 WEB).

"It is my prayer that your love may abound more and more, with knowledge and all discernment, so that you may approve what is excellent, and so be pure and blameless for the day of Christ" (Philippians 1:9–10).

day forty-two

Forever and Ever

There is no friendship, and there is no love, like that of the parent to the child.

Henry Ward Beecher

Whoever receives one such child in my name receives me.

Matthew 18:5

"Do you understand that adoption is a permanent and final decision?"

"Yes. We do."

As the family-court judge asked this question of our son and daughter-in-law, family and friends sniffed and dabbed their eyes. Each person's heart was moved by this truth.

Adoption is permanent. It cannot be undone. It is impossible to reverse or cancel. It is final. In the words of the judge that day, "It is forever and ever."

Forever and ever, Avett will be a deeply cherished member of this family.

Our family has been part of four such ceremonies. We have been blessed to have four grandsons enter our family through adoption.

When Noah, Aiden, Avett, and Xavier joined our family, it seemed as if we had been waiting for these exact little boys. They fit perfectly. Each brought energy, laughter, affection, and their own unique personalities. They bonded immediately with aunts, uncles, and many cousins. Our lives instantly became richer, fuller, and noisier. We can't imagine our family without their smiles and hugs.

Forever and ever these boys will be our boys.

The word *adoption* derives from the Latin *adoptare*—*ad* meaning "to" and *optare* meaning "choose, wish, desire." It literally means "to choose."[29] Adoption signifies a choice. A string of life-giving choices was made before the judge signed the final papers.

Each birth mother chose life. God bless them.

Each birth mother chose our children to be the adoptive parents. What a precious, unselfish gift.

Our children chose to embrace these boys as Jesus would. Along with two other sets of loving grandparents, we are so proud and grateful.

More importantly, God orchestrated every choice that led these children to their new homes. His guidance can be seen in each step along the path.

Adoption has a spiritual dimension. The adoption process and final proclamation reflect God's grand plan for our permanent adoption into His family.

Being the adopted children of God is our destiny. From the beginning, it was God's plan to make us His children. "He predestined us for adoption to himself as sons through Jesus Christ, according to the purpose of his will" (Ephesians 1:5).

He chooses us to be His children.

Our spiritual adoption welcomes us into a much larger family, one that spans the centuries. We bond with brothers and sisters. We receive the full rights of a family member. "To all who did receive him, who believed in his name, he gave the right to become children of God" (John 1:12).

Perhaps the greatest gift of adoption is this—the child now has an attentive Father. When sad or afraid they can call on Daddy. His arms are ready to offer comfort. "And because you are sons, God has sent the Spirit of his Son into our hearts, crying, 'Abba! Father!'" (Galatians 4:6).

When children enter a home through adoption or birth, parents lavish love and attention on the little one. Like a loving Father, God lavishes love on His adopted children. The most lavish expression of love is to call someone your child. "See what great love the Father has lavished on us, that we should be called children of God! And that is what we are!" (1 John 3:1 NIV).

Adoption paints a unique and moving picture of the gospel like nothing else can. Billy Graham and Max Lucado put it beautifully. "God has adopted you. God sought you, found you, signed the papers and took you home."[30]

I pray that as our grandsons mature, they will increasingly cherish their adoptions. May the truth that they were chosen bring joy and security every day of their lives. I pray their own adoptions will give them a clear picture of God's lavish love for them.

I pray all our grandchildren will gain a deep understanding of the gospel as they witness the beauty of adoption within their own family. What a lavish gift we have been given.

Let us pray that . . .

- our grandchildren will believe that God knew them before they were born and has a plan for their lives (Psalm 139:13–16).

- our grandchildren will gain a deep appreciation for adoption (Ephesians 1:5).

- our grandchildren will recognize God as a Father they can call on in times of need (Matthew 6:9–13; Galatians 4:4–7).

- our grandchildren will be grateful for the family God has given them (Exodus 20:12; 1 Thessalonians 5:18).

- our grandchildren will receive Jesus as Savior and become a child of God forever (John 1:12; 1 John 3:1).

Heavenly Father, we thank you for the precious gift of children. Thank you for each one who has entered our families through birth or through adoption. Our hearts are full because of the joy and love they bring. We pray our adopted grandchildren will feel loved, secure, and chosen. Strengthen their bond within the family. Protect their hearts from discouragement and anxiety. Thank you for adopting us as your children. It is an honor to be called a child of God. And that

is what we are. Grant each of our grandchildren hearts that will delight in your lavish love for them. Amen.

Think and Do

- *Chosen for Greatness: How Adoption Changes the World* by Paul J. Batura is a look at the beauty and power of adoption.
- You may not have adopted grandchildren, but you can support children in need. Both World Vision International and Samaritan's Purse have programs that will make a difference in a child's life.
- Read John 1:12–13 and 1 John 3:1. God's love made each of us His child. Reflect on the significance of the lavish love of God and its impact on your daily life. What thoughts do you have about being chosen and adopted forever as His daughter?

"You formed my inward parts; you knitted me together in my mother's womb. I praise you, for I am fearfully and wonderfully made. Wonderful are your works; my soul knows it very well. My frame was not hidden from you, when I was being made in secret, intricately woven in the depths of the earth. Your eyes saw my unformed substance; in your book were written, every one of them, the days that were formed for me, when as yet there was none of them" (Psalm 139:13–16).

"He predestined us for adoption to himself as sons through Jesus Christ, according to the purpose of his will" (Ephesians 1:5).

"Our Father in heaven, hallowed be your name" (Matthew 6:9).

"Because you are sons, God has sent the Spirit of his Son into our hearts, crying, 'Abba! Father!' So you are no longer a slave, but a son, and if a son, then an heir through God" (Galatians 4:6–7).

"Honor your father and your mother, that your days may be long in the land that the LORD your God is giving you" (Exodus 20:12).

"Rejoice always, pray without ceasing, give thanks in all circumstances; for this is the will of God in Christ Jesus for you" (1 Thessalonians 5:16–18).

"To all who did receive him, who believed in his name, he gave the right to become children of God" (John 1:12).

"See what kind of love the Father has given to us, that we should be called children of God; and so we are" (1 John 3:1).

day forty-three

Lean on Me

God desires that we should live in a real, moment-by-moment, total dependence on Him.

Chuck Smith

Trust in the LORD forever, for the LORD GOD is an everlasting rock.

Isaiah 26:4

Like many, I suffer from aerophobia.

To put my life in the hands of an airline pilot I've never met strikes me as absurd. And how do I know whether the mechanic had a stressful morning? Perhaps, while brooding over an argument with his wife, he forgot to tighten a bolt on the wing.

Nevertheless, once the plane starts its climb to thirty thousand feet, I surrender. The full weight of my trust is in the belief that the pilot, engineers, mechanics, and control-tower operators know more about aircraft than I do.

Actually, I know nothing. Soaring through the clouds, I fully rely upon their skill, education, and experience. I sit back and relax. I have no other choice.

Every day presents new opportunities to trust others. Sometimes our dependable people come through for us. At other times, our confidence is misplaced. After all, our loved ones are only frail humans the same as we are.

Life is filled with opportunities to trust in God and His wisdom. Many life events are out of our control. Financial worries, health scares, family conflict, political unrest all leave us feeling depleted and helpless.

God's Word tells us that when our strength is gone or we need guidance and help, we can lean on Him. We can put the full weight of our trust in Him.

Proverbs 3:5–6 is a favorite passage for young Christians. "Trust in the LORD with all your heart, and do not lean on your own understanding. In all your ways acknowledge him, and he will make straight your paths."

Someone said that leaning on our own understanding is like leaning on a broken crutch. Leaning on a broken crutch is foolishness. It won't support our weight. Instead, it will snap, splinter, and send us tumbling. We end up in worse shape than before.

Our own understanding of life (or aeronautics) is often like a broken crutch. It is of no help. Even in our best moments, our understanding is flawed and shaky. To lean too heavily upon our human wisdom would be foolish. We need to shift our weight onto something more dependable.

God can bear the full weight of our sorrows and troubles. He is worthy of all our trust.

Leaning on God is not like leaning on a broken crutch. God's love will never splinter. It will never snap. It will never slip out from under us. It will never send us tumbling helter-skelter.

His wisdom is sure and far greater than our own (Isaiah 55:8–9). Our trust can safely rest on Him. Unlike a broken crutch, God's love can bear our full weight.

When we need to lean on something for support, cardboard, flimsy material, or wobbly furniture won't do. We search for something that is solid, certain, and unmovable.

God is our rock. He is unmovable. We can lean on Him without fear of falling or being let down. We can lean on Him continually. "Be to me a rock of refuge, to which I may continually come; you have given the command to save me, for you are my rock and my fortress" (Psalm 71:3).

Too often, we trust in our own broken-down, shaky understanding and thinking. We assume we are wise enough to figure life out ourselves. Maybe it is time to throw away that broken, risky crutch.

How much better to admit that God always knows more than we do. We can trust Him completely. We can lean on Him without fear. He is our rock.

I pray my grandchildren will learn early in life to resist relying only on their own understanding. I pray they will humbly admit their need for God's wisdom. May they totally depend upon Him for guidance, strength, and help. May they put the full weight of their trust in the knowledge that He knows more than they do.

Let us pray that . . .

- our grandchildren will not lean on their own understanding (Proverbs 3:5–6).
- our grandchildren will not trust in their own minds alone but seek wisdom (Proverbs 28:26).
- our grandchildren will fully trust in God even when afraid (Psalm 56:3).
- our grandchildren will trust in the Lord forever (Isaiah 26:4).
- our grandchildren will believe God's ways are superior to man's (Isaiah 55:8–9).
- our grandchildren will be humble and allow God to teach them (Psalm 25:4).

Heavenly Father, our pride says that we know all the answers. We don't. Forgive us for trusting ourselves more than we trust you. Life has taught us that when we lean on you, we find true peace. We want to totally depend upon you. We pray that our grandchildren will lean on you and not on themselves. Teach them that you are the only one they can completely trust. May they learn early that you are wise and

good and ready to help them. We pray they will never hesitate to run to you, their rock and fortress. Amen.

Think and Do

- Read Psalm 71:3. Is leaning on God and trusting Him fully a onetime deal? C. S. Lewis wrote, "Relying on God has to begin all over again every day as if nothing had yet been done."[31] How can you make continually leaning on God part of your life?

- By your words and actions, encourage your grandchildren to lean upon God. David is a well-known example of a man who leaned on God in difficult times. Read the stories of David and Psalm 20:7 with your grandchildren and discuss what things people rely upon today instead of leaning on God.

"Trust in the LORD with all your heart, and do not lean on your own understanding. In all your ways acknowledge him, and he will make straight your paths" (Proverbs 3:5–6).

"Whoever trusts in his own mind is a fool, but he who walks in wisdom will be delivered" (Proverbs 28:26).

"When I am afraid, I put my trust in you" (Psalm 56:3).

"Trust in the LORD forever, for the LORD GOD is an everlasting rock" (Isaiah 26:4).

"My thoughts are not your thoughts, neither are your ways my ways, declares the LORD. For as the heavens are higher than the earth, so are my ways higher than your ways and my thoughts than your thoughts" (Isaiah 55:8–9).

"Make me to know your ways, O LORD; teach me your paths" (Psalm 25:4).

day forty-four

Jolabokaflod

Books are not made for furniture, but there is nothing else that so beautifully furnishes a house.

Henry Ward Beecher

Let the words of my mouth and the meditation of my heart be acceptable in your sight, O LORD, my rock and my redeemer.

Psalm 19:14

Every November Iceland's publishers mail a catalog of new releases to every literature-loving home. Moms and dads, grandmas and grandpas, brothers and sisters, and close friends flip through the glossy pages. Each is seeking the perfect gift for the bookworm in their life.

This Icelandic tradition is known as Jolabokaflod—the Christmas flood of books.

Christmas book giving began during World War II. Dairy, sugar, meat, coffee, and other household and personal items were strictly rationed. But not paper. Books became the perfect (and perhaps the only) Christmas gift.

Icelanders open their gifts on Christmas Eve. With a warm cup of cocoa in one hand and a new book in the other, each family member spends a cozy Christmas Eve curled up with their gift. This is a tradition we all could embrace.

During our children's preschool and elementary years, I frequently leafed through *Honey for a Child's Heart* by Gladys Hunt. I've never forgotten her words at the end of chapter one. "Young children, fresh uncluttered minds, the world before them—to what treasures will you lead them? With what will you furnish their spirit?"[32]

Moved by the possibility of furnishing my children's (and grandchildren's) spirits with the wonder of children's literature, I filled shelves and already bulging boxes with whatever I could find. I longed to feed their souls with honey.

Each child had favorites. *Too-Loose the Chocolate Moose* was always a winner. The Little Bear series, *Honey Rabbit*, the Chronicles of Narnia series, *Charlie and the Chocolate Factory*, any books about horses, and dozens of Bible stories became part of our daily lives. Our children loved story time, but it had an unexpected bonus. We bonded as we laughed together at *The Monster at the End of This Book* or marveled at the bravery of David. Those were the best moments of my life.

Literature shapes our thinking and worldview. It encourages character development without preaching.

Author Sarah Clarkson believes good children's literature is essential to moral development. "The plain yet nuanced language of the children's classics constantly shapes child readers by helping them to notice what is lovely, to love what is beautiful, and to value what is loyal and true."[33]

Why is this so important?

Ours is an entertainment-obsessed culture. Every day children are bombarded with stories, images, and music designed to shape how they think and control what they value as good. The ideals and virtues that will prepare them for life are often absent. Worse, these precious virtues are often dismissed.

In Psalm 101:2–3, David reaffirms his commitment to God. He writes of how he will manage his life at home. "I will walk with integrity of heart within my house; I will not set before my eyes anything that is worthless." David understood the danger of gazing on worthless things. Taking in useless things would compromise his integrity. They possessed the power to damage his relationship with God.

Compare David's words in Psalm 101 with his heartfelt prayer in Psalm 19:14: "Let the words of my mouth and the meditation of my heart be acceptable in your sight, O LORD, my rock and my redeemer."

The New Testament tells us to choose what we think. To do that, we must certainly choose what we read and watch.

"Whatever is true, whatever is honorable, whatever is just, whatever is pure, whatever is lovely, whatever is commendable, if there is any excellence, if there is anything worthy of praise, think about these things" (Philippians 4:8).

We have no control over the moral blitz aimed at children. But we can gently offer our grandchildren more honorable ways of thinking by giving them the gift of children's literature. We have the opportunity to furnish their spirits with noble tales of adventure, bravery, honesty, and sacrifice. There is a bonus. Over stories, we bond with the little people in our lives.

We have the joy of offering "honey for a child's heart."

I pray that our grandchildren will fall in love with good and honorable stories. May the Lord use tales of honesty and sacrifice to nurture their character and fill them with courage and determination.

Let us pray that . . .

- our grandchildren's choices in literature, art, and music will honor God (Colossians 3:17).

- our grandchildren will keep themselves unpolluted by the world (James 1:27).

- our grandchildren will avoid worthless things and thoughts (Psalm 101:3).

- our grandchildren's thoughts will be acceptable in God's sight (Psalm 19:14).

- our grandchildren will fill their minds with what is lovely and honorable (Philippians 4:8).

- our grandchildren will use their own creative gifts to glorify God (Colossians 3:23).

Heavenly Father, we thank you for the beauty of literature. So many stories help us to look at the world with fresh eyes and see your goodness. Lord, protect our grandchildren from the negativity of media in every form. Help us to be humble examples of guarding what we watch, see, read, and hear. Lead them to literature, music, and art that will thrill their souls. We pray for the young artists in our families. May they take on the mission of writing, singing, drawing, dancing, instrumental music, craftsmanship, and drama for your glory. Amen.

Think and Do

- Not all children enjoy reading. But all children love stories. If you have a reluctant reader in the family, audiobooks are a good option. If you have a long-distance grandchild, reading to them via a device is a great alternative.

- Both *Honey for a Child's Heart* by Gladys Hunt and *Caught Up in a Story* by Sarah Clarkson offer lists of books that you may find helpful.

- What was your favorite book as a child? Did a particular piece of children's literature shape your thinking or teach you a lesson you've not forgotten?

"Whatever you do, in word or deed, do everything in the name of the Lord Jesus, giving thanks to God the Father through him" (Colossians 3:17).

"Religion that is pure and undefiled before God the Father is this: to visit orphans and widows in their affliction, and to keep oneself unstained from the world" (James 1:27).

"I will not set before my eyes anything that is worthless. I hate the work of those who fall away; it shall not cling to me" (Psalm 101:3).

"Let the words of my mouth and the meditation of my heart be acceptable in your sight, O LORD, my rock and my redeemer" (Psalm 19:14).

"Whatever is true, whatever is honorable, whatever is just, whatever is pure, whatever is lovely, whatever is commendable, if there is any excellence, if there is anything worthy of praise, think about these things" (Philippians 4:8).

"Whatever you do, work heartily, as for the Lord and not for men" (Colossians 3:23).

day forty-five

Marriage Is a Treasure

The man who loves his wife above all else on earth gains the freedom and power to pursue other noble, but lesser, loves.

David Jeremiah

Let marriage be held in honor among all.

Hebrews 13:4

The one-hundred-year-old vase sits on our buffet. It was hand painted by my grandmother in the early 1900s. This vase is a treasured possession. In the spring, I fill it with multicolored tulips. Daisies enhance its rustic look in the summer.

This family heirloom has been passed on to me. My job is to lovingly protect the vase and its history until it someday finds a new home.

When we treasure something, we lovingly care for and protect it. We shield it and keep it out of harm's way. When we treat an object as a treasure, we affirm the prized object or person.

If you are married, perhaps you remember standing at the altar as you said your vows. Eyes locked, turned toward one another, you pledged yourself to love, honor, and cherish each other. Then you exchanged rings to seal the vow.

Two years ago, my husband and I attended a marriage seminar led by Gary Thomas. The entire workshop was built around one word: *cherish*. As we later purchased his book, *Cherish: The One Word That*

Changes Everything for Your Marriage, our hearts were touched by the truth of that title. "Cherish is the melody that makes a marriage sing."[34]

On the day a couple makes their sincere vows, each believes their spouse will cherish them, guaranteeing a happily ever after. They leave the ceremony with high hopes and great dreams. When cherishing is lacking in a marriage, the disappointment is crushing.

Just as I cherish and treasure Grandma's vase, we all must tenderly treasure, cherish, prize, and value our spouses. I promise you, it changes everything.

Our culture no longer "cherishes" the idea of marriage. We no longer protect the idea of marriage. It has lost its value.

Throughout history, every society has viewed marriage as honorable. Each new marriage was a cause for celebration. A wedding symbolized the natural progression of life. The transition from childhood to adulthood was complete. Every culture applauded the creation of a new family as healthy and of value to the entire community.

That has changed. For many, marriage is unnecessary.

A *U.S. News & World Report* article reveals the changing face of marriage. Thirty-five percent of men and thirty percent of women have never been married. In 1949, seventy-eight percent of households were made up of married couples. In 2019 that number fell to forty-eight percent.[35]

Due to financial concerns and society's negativity, marriage is on a steep decline.

For some, marriage is outdated and represents a loss of freedom. Others argue that marriage is an oppressive institution.

The Bible has a different opinion.

From the earliest chapters, we see that God created marriage for our welfare and for His glory. "Then the LORD God said, 'It is not good that the man should be alone'" (Genesis 2:18). Verse 24 gives us God's remedy for man's aloneness: "Therefore a man shall leave his father and his mother and hold fast to his wife, and they shall become one flesh."

Marriage was the perfect cure for Adam's loneliness. God intended marriage to be a source of delight.

The writer of Hebrews encouraged a high view of marriage: "Let marriage be held in honor among all" (Hebrews 13:4). I think we could assume the writer "cherished" the idea of marriage.

Marriage is a metaphor for Christ and the church. "'Therefore a man shall leave his father and mother and hold fast to his wife, and the two shall become one flesh.' This mystery is profound, and I am saying that it refers to Christ and the church" (Ephesians 5:31–32).

Marriage is sacred, honorable, beautiful, symbolic, and meets our needs. It has been given to us by a generous God. It is our job to lovingly shield, protect, and guard it as the treasure it is. It is our job to champion the idea of marriage as a precious gift.

Marriage is worth cherishing.

We may be married, single, divorced, widowed, remarried. Perhaps we are about to celebrate our fiftieth anniversary. No matter our current experience, we have the opportunity and obligation to verbally place high value on biblical marriage.

I want my grandchildren to have a vision for marriage that is in keeping with God's Word. I hope they will treasure this holy covenant. I pray they will reject the world's attitude toward marriage. May they embrace the biblical view and become cheerleaders for marriage.

I also pray that their own marriages will delight their souls and demonstrate the sweet power of "cherishing" one another.

Let us pray that . . .

- our grandchildren will seek God's will for marriage (Luke 22:42).
- our grandchildren will embrace marriage as a lifelong commitment to one person (Genesis 2:24; Mark 10:6–7).
- our grandchildren will honor marriage and maintain its purity (Hebrews 13:4).
- our grandchildren will marry like-minded people (2 Corinthians 6:14).
- our grandchildren will love sacrificially and show respect (Ephesians 5:24–27, 33).
- our grandchildren will be humble and patient with their spouses (Ephesians 4:32).
- our grandchildren will have marriages that bring them great delight (Song of Solomon 4:9).

Heavenly Father, it is our desire to honor marriage as your creation. Forgive us for neglecting to care for, protect, and treasure the institution of marriage. Help us to honor our vows to love, honor, and cherish. We pray for a revival of loving marriages in our homes, churches, nation, and world. May every member of the church, married or not, be cheerleaders for loving marriages. Give our grandchildren a vision of a life-giving marriage. May their marriages be a delight and an honor to you. Amen.

Think and Do

- *Before You Split: Find What You Really Want for the Future of Your Marriage* by Toni Nieuwhof is an excellent and hopeful resource for a friend or family member on the brink of divorce.
- *Cherish: The One Word That Changes Everything for Your Marriage* by Gary Thomas inspires and encourages married couples to remember their vows to cherish one another. Gary's suggestions and illustrations can breathe new life and joy into your relationship, no matter how long you have been married. It is an excellent gift book.
- Are you a cheerleader for biblical marriage? How can you help your grandchildren have a high view of marriage? "Let marriage be held in honor among all" (Hebrews 13:4).

"Not my will, but yours, be done" (Luke 22:42).

"Therefore a man shall leave his father and his mother and hold fast to his wife, and they shall become one flesh" (Genesis 2:24).

"From the beginning of creation, 'God made them male and female.' 'Therefore a man shall leave his father and mother and hold fast to his wife, and the two shall become one flesh'" (Mark 10:6–8).

"Let marriage be held in honor among all, and let the marriage bed be undefiled, for God will judge the sexually immoral and adulterous" (Hebrews 13:4).

"Do not be unequally yoked with unbelievers. For what partnership has righteousness with lawlessness? Or what fellowship has light with darkness?" (2 Corinthians 6:14).

"Now as the church submits to Christ, so also wives should submit in everything to their husbands. Husbands, love your wives, as Christ loved the church and gave himself up for her, that he might sanctify her, having cleansed her by the washing of water with the word, so that he might present the church to himself in splendor, without spot or wrinkle or any such thing, that she might be holy and without blemish. . . . Let each one of you love his wife as himself, and let the wife see that she respects her husband" (Ephesians 5:24–27, 33).

"Be kind to one another, tenderhearted, forgiving one another, as God in Christ forgave you" (Ephesians 4:32).

"You have captivated my heart, my sister, my bride; you have captivated my heart with one glance of your eyes, with one jewel of your necklace" (Song of Solomon 4:9).

day forty-six

Rock of Ages

Be of sin the double cure: save from wrath and make me pure.

Augustus Toplady

Since, therefore, we have now been justified by his blood, much more shall we be saved by him from the wrath of God.

Romans 5:9

Do you feel blessed by modern medicine? Illnesses that once reduced the quality of life for our grandparents are now managed with both old and new medications and treatments. Life expectancy grows by leaps and bounds.

Aspirin is a wonder drug. It treats more than one problem. It prevents heart attacks and soothes headaches. Beta blockers lower blood pressure and quiet the heart rate. Allergies flaring up? Try an antihistamine and enjoy the bonus of a good night's sleep.

You could call these drugs "double cures." They treat more than one problem.

In 1762, Augustus Toplady authored the familiar hymn, "Rock of Ages." According to a well-known legend, Toplady wrote the hymn while sheltering from a storm in Burrington Combe. A plaque marks the spot in the gorge where it is said Toplady hid for safety.

"Rock of Ages: This rock derives its name from the well-known hymn written about 1762 by the Rev. A. M. Toplady who was inspired whilst sheltering in this cleft during a storm."[36]

Some argue that the event never occurred. Even so, the rock, appearing to be nearly split in two by a long fissure, provided a perfect shelter where a traveler could hide and find protection.

> Rock of Ages, cleft for me,
> Let me hide myself in thee;
> Let the water and the blood,
> From thy wounded side which flowed,
> *Be of sin the double cure;*
> *Save from wrath and make me pure.* (emphasis added)[37]

Hidden and secure in the cleft of the rock, Toplady cries out—not for safety from a thunderstorm—but for a "double cure" from sin. It isn't enough just to be saved from wrath. And it isn't enough just to be forgiven. He needed something that would treat both problems. He believed that the blood of Jesus could do both, and more.

It is Jesus who saves us from the wrath to come. "You turned to God from idols to serve the living and true God, and to wait for his Son from heaven, whom he raised from the dead, Jesus who delivers us from the wrath to come" (1 Thessalonians 1:9–10).

Our destiny is not wrath, but salvation through Jesus Christ. "For God has not destined us for wrath, but to obtain salvation through our Lord Jesus Christ" (1 Thessalonians 5:9).

Because of Jesus, salvation, not wrath, is our destiny.

The blood also cures and cleans up our moral sickness.

Jesus cleanses our souls, scours away all unrighteousness. "If we confess our sins, he is faithful and just to forgive us our sins and to cleanse us from all unrighteousness" (1 John 1:9).

The matchless blood of Jesus even purifies our consciences. "How much more will the blood of Christ, who through the eternal Spirit offered himself without blemish to God, purify our conscience from dead works to serve the living God" (Hebrews 9:14).

In Revelation 1:5, the apostle John gives praise to the one who makes us pure, "to him who loves us and has freed us from our sins by his blood."

The blood of Jesus surpasses the "double cure" hoped for by Augustus Toplady. It is a wonder medicine that cures many ills.

Hebrews 10:19 tells us that "we have confidence to enter the holy places by the blood of Jesus." Isaiah 53:5 tells us that we will someday experience complete healing because of the blood of Christ. "He was pierced for our transgressions; he was crushed for our iniquities; upon him was the chastisement that brought us peace, and with his wounds we are healed."

The blood of Jesus is a miracle cure. I guess you could say it is a spiritual "cure-all."

There is real peace in knowing that Jesus has provided a "double cure" for our sin. My prayer is that my grandchildren will understand the efficacy of the blood of Christ and live in freedom and joy. May they make an appointment with the Great Physician who can cure all their ills.

Let us pray that . . .

- our grandchildren will know that the church is precious and was bought with the blood of Jesus (Acts 20:28).

- our grandchildren will know that Jesus came to reconcile and make peace with all things through His blood (Colossians 1:20).

- our grandchildren will believe that their destiny is salvation and not wrath (1 Thessalonians 5:9).

- our grandchildren will believe that if they confess their sins, Jesus will forgive and purify (1 John 1:9).

- our grandchildren will be made holy by the blood of Jesus (Hebrews 13:12).

- our grandchildren will rejoice that they are free from condemnation because of the blood of Jesus (Romans 8:1).

Heavenly Father, we thank you for the priceless, precious blood of Jesus. Because of His blood we escape the wrath to come. Because of His sacrifice we have redemption and are purified. We pray that our grandchildren will seek the "double cure" for their sins. May your

Holy Spirit convict them of their need and convince them of the power of the blood of Christ. May they live in freedom as they grasp that there is "no condemnation for those who are in Christ Jesus" (Romans 8:1). Amen.

Think and Do

- Read and meditate on 1 Peter 1:17–19. "If you call on him as Father who judges impartially according to each one's deeds, conduct yourselves with fear throughout the time of your exile, knowing that you were ransomed from the futile ways inherited from your forefathers, not with perishable things such as silver or gold, but with the precious blood of Christ, like that of a lamb without blemish or spot." From what have you been delivered? Reflect on the price that was paid for your redemption.

- *Little Pilgrim's Progress* (illustrated edition) by Helen L. Taylor is an adaptation of John Bunyan's classic *Pilgrim's Progress*. It tells of Little Christian's journey in a way that is suitable for children ages eight to twelve. Thousands have found encouragement for their own spiritual journeys through this classic work.

"Pay careful attention to yourselves and to all the flock, in which the Holy Spirit has made you overseers, to care for the church of God, which he obtained with his own blood" (Acts 20:28).

"In him all the fullness of God was pleased to dwell, and through him to reconcile to himself all things, whether on earth or in heaven, making peace by the blood of his cross" (Colossians 1:19–20).

"God has not destined us for wrath, but to obtain salvation through our Lord Jesus Christ" (1 Thessalonians 5:9).

"If we confess our sins, he is faithful and just to forgive us our sins and to cleanse us from all unrighteousness" (1 John 1:9).

"Jesus also suffered outside the city gate to make the people holy through his own blood" (Hebrews 13:12 NIV).

"There is therefore now no condemnation for those who are in Christ Jesus" (Romans 8:1).

day forty-seven

Like the Sky

A teardrop on earth summons the King of Heaven.

Chuck Swindoll

Rejoice with those who rejoice, weep with those who weep.

Romans 12:15

C. S. Lewis was no stranger to sorrow.

In *A Grief Observed*, Lewis described the depression he suffered after the loss of his wife, Joy. "Her absence is like the sky, spread over everything."[38]

Grief, sorrow, and worry spread. The happiest occasions can be clouded by a passing shadow of sorrow.

Author Donne Davis, in her book *When Being a Grandma Isn't So Grand,* writes about the women in the grandmother groups she organizes and leads. She has observed that for some "it is too painful to attend our meetings because of the conflicts they face in their relationships with the parents of their grandchildren."[39]

Some grandparents know too well the pain of strained relationships. Friction and conflict bleed into every area. Many of life's events become bittersweet.

Some grandparents experience physical, emotional, or spiritual distance from children and grandchildren. Others pace the floor as health, relational, or financial issues ambush the family.

Many weep for the prodigal child or grandchild who has yet to come home. The loss of a grandchild by death devastates. Grief punches a hole in the heart that can never be filled.

Helpless, many grandparents watch as their children and grandchildren endure the trauma of divorce and ugly custody battles. They experience shock as the family unit crumbles.

Some grandparents suffer financial pain. With retirement approaching, caring for grandchildren can shrink the bank account. Many grandparents count the financial and physical cost of providing stability for grandchildren. They gladly pay the price, but there is a price.

There is no joy like family joy. There is no pain like family pain.

Like the sky, our concerns, fears, and grief "spread over everything." Our worries follow us wherever we go.

Someone has said, "No one should ever mourn alone." This is true. It is even more true that grandparents are never alone in their heartaches. God is with us. He sees every tear. His presence and love spread over everything.

> The Lord is near to the brokenhearted and saves the crushed in spirit. (Psalm 34:18)

> When you pass through the waters, I will be with you; and through the rivers, they shall not overwhelm you. (Isaiah 43:2)

> Never will I leave you; never will I forsake you. (Hebrews 13:5 NIV)

> You have kept count of my tossings; put my tears in your bottle. Are they not in your book? (Psalm 56:8)

We are also not alone because God has given us the gift of brothers and sisters in Christ.

In Romans 12:15, Paul laid out an expectation and command for Christian relationships: "Rejoice with those who rejoice, weep with those who weep." When sad, worried, or frustrated with family situations, we should find comfort, encouragement, and support in the body of believers.

We often avoid exactly what we need. We assume no one will understand our dilemma. We are convinced we are alone. No one can offer hope for our unique situation. Isolation intensifies our pain. We need comfort.

Paul offers us a reminder of the comfort offered by both the Comforter and the comforted.

> Blessed be the God and Father of our Lord Jesus Christ, the Father of mercies and God of all comfort, who comforts us in *all* our affliction, so that we may be able to comfort those who are in *any* affliction, with the comfort with which we ourselves are comforted by God. (2 Corinthians 1:3–4, emphasis added)

All and any. In Jesus there is comfort for *all* and *any* of our afflictions. No exceptions. Because Jesus comforts us, we become comforters.

Do you know hurting grandmothers? Weep with them. Remind them that Jesus is present for all and any of their concerns.

Are you a grandmother facing challenges today? Remember God is with you. He can comfort you in all and any of your afflictions. Reach out to your sisters in Christ for comfort. You can be sure that many have endured similar hurt and found hope.

Let us pray for the millions of grandparents who are facing challenges today. Let us ask the Lord to encourage them and strengthen them as they faithfully pray for their grandchildren. May grandmothers and grandchildren alike know that Jesus is near and able to help in their need.

May the love, comfort, and presence of God be like the sky, spreading hope over everything.

Let us pray that . . .

- we will be comforted knowing God is always with us (Isaiah 41:10; Hebrews 13:5).
- we will carry our children and grandchildren to Jesus when the need is great (Luke 5:17–20).
- we will allow the God of all mercy to be our comfort in any and all situations (2 Corinthians 1:3–4).

- we will sincerely rejoice with those who rejoice and weep with those who weep (Romans 12:15).

- we will have Christian brothers and sisters who will love us in adversity (Proverbs 17:17).

- our grandchildren will turn to God, our refuge and strength, in the hard times (Psalm 46:1–2).

- our grandchildren will experience the nearness and comfort of God (Psalm 34:18).

- our grandchildren will take their burdens to Jesus and find rest (Matthew 11:28).

Heavenly Father, you see our tears. You know our fears. You take note of every heartache. We believe your mercy can comfort us—and our families—in any and all of our afflictions. Help us to move from self-pity and isolation into the fellowship of other believers. We pray for hurting grandparents. May their hearts be soothed and healed by your love. Spread your love like the sky over us all. Amen.

Think and Do

- Legacy Coalition provides educational resources and support for grandparents. You can download the mp3 of "Hope for the Hurting Grandparent" from their resources page on their website, www.legacycoalition.com. The presenter, Larry Fowler, offers wisdom and encouragement for grandparents in distress.

- Have you ever noticed how often parents brought children to Jesus (Matthew 17:14–20; Mark 5:21–43; 10:13)? He never turned them away.

"Fear not, for I am with you; be not dismayed, for I am your God; I will strengthen you, I will help you, I will uphold you with my righteous right hand" (Isaiah 41:10).

"Keep your life free from love of money, and be content with what you have, for he has said, 'I will never leave you nor forsake you'" (Hebrews 13:5).

"Some men were bringing on a bed a man who was paralyzed, and they were seeking to bring him in and lay him before Jesus, but finding no way to bring him in, because of the crowd, they went up on the roof and let him down with his bed through the tiles into the midst before Jesus. And when he saw their faith, he said, 'Man, your sins are forgiven you'" (Luke 5:18–20).

"Blessed be the God and Father of our Lord Jesus Christ, the Father of mercies and God of all comfort, who comforts us in all our affliction, so that we may be able to comfort those who are in any affliction, with the comfort with which we ourselves are comforted by God" (2 Corinthians 1:3–4).

"Rejoice with those who rejoice, weep with those who weep" (Romans 12:15).

"A friend loves at all times, and a brother is born for adversity" (Proverbs 17:17).

"God is our refuge and strength, a very present help in trouble. Therefore we will not fear though the earth gives way, though the mountains be moved into the heart of the sea" (Psalm 46:1–2).

"The LORD is near to the brokenhearted and saves the crushed in spirit" (Psalm 34:18).

"Come to me, all you who are weary and burdened, and I will give you rest" (Matthew 11:28 NIV).

day forty-eight

Tip of the Hat

From Genesis to Revelation, here's the central message:
God Almighty, the Lord Jesus Christ, the Spirit of God,
the Triune God is in control of all things, period.

Charles Stanley

Trust in the LORD with all your heart,
and do not lean on your own understanding.
In all your ways acknowledge him,
and he will make straight your paths.

Proverbs 3:5-6

Fedora, bowler, Stetson, beanie.

At one time headgear was an indispensable part of a masculine wardrobe. Now, images of hat-wearing men, offering a tip of their hat to ladies on the street, exist only in old movies. Occasionally, we see a modern-day cowboy give a nod of the head and a tip of the hat. It is charming.

A tip of the hat is a sign of acknowledgment. It is a gesture of respect and value. It communicates, "I see you. You matter. You are valuable."

It is also an expression of thanks. When a batter hits a grand slam home run, he often waves his hat at the cheering crowd in gratitude for their support.

Today, acknowledging another person can be as simple as a nod from across the room. Or it can be as familiar as a friendly fist bump. Either way, our acknowledgment sends the message that this person is valued.

In Proverbs 3:6, we are commanded to acknowledge God. But is our acknowledgment of God the same as tipping our hat to Him? Do we simply nod our head at God and move on with our day?

The word *acknowledge* carries another layer of meaning that helps us to understand what the writer of Proverbs intended. To acknowledge is "to recognize the rights, authority, or status of."[40] When we acknowledge God, we recognize He is the supreme authority, the Sovereign of the universe.

When we acknowledge God, we declare His lordship over every aspect of our lives.

When quoting Proverbs 3:5–6, our mind quickly jumps to the phrase, "he will make straight your paths." We put the cart before the horse.

Before God directs and straightens our paths, we must acknowledge His sovereignty. Not with a mere tip of the hat, but with a heart that knows and trusts Him fully. We remove our hats and bow before Him in reverence and submission.

Cultivating a humble heart allows us to challenge our own limited understanding. When we admit our need, we take the first step in acknowledging God. We concede that God's laws and ways are always superior to our own.

"For my thoughts are not your thoughts, neither are your ways my ways, declares the LORD. For as the heavens are higher than the earth, so are my ways higher than your ways and my thoughts than your thoughts" (Isaiah 55:8–9).

We don't run from God's authority and wisdom. We surrender to it.

It is futile to ask God to lead us when we are determined to chart our own course. Those who resist acknowledging the superiority of God's ways are traveling a bumpy path. (Read the book of Jonah.) Those who acknowledge, trust, and surrender to His wisdom experience the joy of being led by God himself.

It is a struggle for many to acknowledge God. Even when He reveals himself in a sunrise, a spectacular fall day, the love of a family member, the laughter of a friend, or a Bible verse that speaks to a deep need, they seem to miss Him.

How I wish we all would doff our hats and wave at Him in endless gratitude.

I pray I will grow in my understanding of how to acknowledge and cherish God as the ultimate authority. I pray frequently and fervently that my children and grandchildren will own Him as the Sovereign Lord over every area of life. May they continually take notice of His loving presence, surrender to Him, and find His straight paths for their lives.

Let us pray that . . .

- our grandchildren will bow before the Sovereign Lord in every area of life (Psalm 95:6).
- our grandchildren will acknowledge the sovereignty of God before asking for direction (Proverbs 3:5–7).
- our grandchildren will seek God first and trust Him for all their needs (Matthew 6:33).
- our grandchildren will commit themselves to doing God's will and living for His kingdom (Matthew 6:9–13).
- our grandchildren will realize that everything they do is for the Lord and not for themselves (Colossians 3:17).
- our grandchildren will honor Jesus as Lord (1 Peter 3:15).

Heavenly Father, we acknowledge that you are the ultimate authority. We yield to you as Sovereign God over all things. Lord, we pray that our grandchildren will know you thoroughly. May they learn to acknowledge your authority before asking for direction. May they yield to the lordship of Christ. We pray they will experience the joy of being led on the paths you prepare for them. Amen.

Think and Do

- Many women have found the teachings in *Surrender: The Heart God Controls* by Nancy Leigh DeMoss to be helpful for thinking through the neglected issue of surrender.

- In Matthew 10, Jesus tells the disciples He is sending them out like sheep among wolves. He instructs them not to be afraid of those who oppose the truth: "Whoever acknowledges me before others, I will also acknowledge before my Father in heaven" (v. 32 NIV). How is this passage relevant today? Do you ever hesitate to acknowledge God before your grandchildren? What comfort and motivation does this passage offer you?

"Oh come, let us worship and bow down; let us kneel before the LORD, our Maker!" (Psalm 95:6).

"Trust in the LORD with all your heart, and do not lean on your own understanding. In all your ways acknowledge him, and he will make straight your paths" (Proverbs 3:5–6).

"Seek first the kingdom of God and his righteousness, and all these things will be added to you" (Matthew 6:33).

"Our Father in heaven, hallowed be your name. Your kingdom come, your will be done, on earth as it is in heaven. Give us this day our daily bread, and forgive us our debts, as we also have forgiven our debtors. And lead us not into temptation, but deliver us from evil" (Matthew 6:9–13).

"Whatever you do, in word or deed, do everything in the name of the Lord Jesus, giving thanks to God the Father through him" (Colossians 3:17).

"In your hearts honor Christ the Lord as holy, always being prepared to make a defense to anyone who asks you for a reason for the hope that is in you; yet do it with gentleness and respect" (1 Peter 3:15).

day forty-nine

Enough Character

The fellow that has no money is poor. The fellow that has nothing but money is poorer still.

Billy Sunday

> Give me neither poverty nor riches;
> feed me with the food that is needful for me.
>
> Proverbs 30:8

Kevin and Viv Nicholson hit the jackpot.

Viv worked in a cake factory in Castleford, England. Her husband spent his nights in a dark and dusty coal mine. Chronically strapped for cash, they struggled to put food on the table for their three children.

Viv and Kevin wagered a few meager shillings on an upcoming soccer game. On April 11, 1961, the shocked couple won the Littlewoods Football Pool. What a windfall! The couple took home £152,000 (more than $4.5 million today).

When asked about her plans, the flamboyant Viv exclaimed, "Spend, spend, spend."

And that is precisely what she did. In just a few years, the money was gone.[41]

A bonanza of cash should provide lifelong security. It rarely does.

A wise man by the name of Agur saw the dangers of both poverty and riches. In Proverbs 30:7–9 he makes an unusual request of the Lord.

> Two things I ask of you;
>   deny them not to me before I die:
> Remove far from me falsehood and lying;
>   give me neither poverty nor riches;

feed me with the food that is needful for me,
    lest I be full and deny you
        and say, "Who is the LORD?"
    or lest I be poor and steal
        and profane the name of my God.

Being aware of his own weaknesses may have been Agur's greatest strength. The self-aware writer of this proverb understood that both poverty and riches posed a danger to his soul.

If he became rich, he might become self-reliant, complacent, arrogant. Trusting wealth for security, he would feel no need for God. Denying God would be a real danger.

If he were poor, he might become bitter. Living hand to mouth, would he doubt God's goodness? Would he be tempted to make moral compromises to get what he wanted? The consequences would be catastrophic. He would dishonor God's name.

Author and Bible teacher Jan Silvious boils down Agur's prayer for us. "Lord, don't overpower me with too much because I don't have enough character to handle it. And, Lord, don't deprive me of too much because I don't have enough character to handle it."[42]

Managing both poverty and riches requires solid character. We need character more than we need riches.

I shared this verse with my oldest grandchild. At the end of our conversation, we agreed we should only ask for that which we can "manage" well.

My prayer for my grandchildren is for neither poverty nor riches. I pray they will be given what is needful. I also pray that they will develop enough humility and character to handle the sticky situations of life. May they only be given what they can manage well—with grace and faith in the goodness of God.

Let us pray that . . .

- our grandchildren will understand that life does not consist of abundant possessions (Luke 12:15).

- our grandchildren will put their faith in the God who richly provides (1 Timothy 6:17).

- our grandchildren will trust God to supply every need (Philippians 4:19).
- our grandchildren will be content with few possessions and much righteousness (Proverbs 16:8).
- our grandchildren will develop the character they need to persevere in life (Romans 5:4).
- our grandchildren will have hearts like the widow, who gave out of her poverty, and Joseph of Arimathea, who gave out of his abundance (Mark 12:42–44; John 19:38–42).

Heavenly Father, absolutely everything we have comes from your hand. We do not ask for great riches. We don't have enough character to manage it. We ask you to protect us from the poverty that might cause us to doubt you. We don't have enough character to manage it. Lord, give our grandchildren just what they need to be content. Give them enough character to manage whatever you give. Amen.

Think and Do

- *The Children's Book of Virtues* by William Bennett continues to be a favorite with families. Stories from around the world entertain and encourage children to embrace character traits that make for a rich and fulfilling life.
- Agur's prayer sprang from a humble heart. Read and reflect on 1 Peter 5:6–7 and Colossians 3:12.
- Thousands have found financial help through Financial Peace University. If your grandchild's parents are looking for a way to teach their children about finances, *Financial Peace Jr.* is a great starting point.

"He said to them, 'Take care, and be on your guard against all covetousness, for one's life does not consist in the abundance of his possessions'" (Luke 12:15).

"As for the rich in this present age, charge them not to be haughty, nor to set their hopes on the uncertainty of riches, but on God, who richly provides us with everything to enjoy. They are to do good, to be rich in good works, to be generous and ready to share, thus storing up treasure for themselves as a good foundation for the future, so that they may take hold of that which is truly life" (1 Timothy 6:17–19).

"My God will supply every need of yours according to his riches in glory in Christ Jesus" (Philippians 4:19).

"Better is a little with righteousness than great revenues with injustice" (Proverbs 16:8).

"Not only that, but we rejoice in our sufferings, knowing that suffering produces endurance, and endurance produces character, and character produces hope" (Romans 5:3–4).

"After these things Joseph of Arimathea, who was a disciple of Jesus, but secretly for fear of the Jews, asked Pilate that he might take away the body of Jesus, and Pilate gave him permission. So he came and took away his body. Nicodemus also, who earlier had come to Jesus by night, came bringing a mixture of myrrh and aloes, about seventy-five pounds in weight. So they took the body of Jesus and bound it in linen cloths with the spices, as is the burial custom of the Jews. Now in the place where he was crucified there was a garden, and in the garden a new tomb in which no one had yet been laid. . . . They laid Jesus there" (John 19:38–42).

"A poor widow came and put in two small copper coins, which make a penny. And he called his disciples to him and said to them, 'Truly, I say to you, this poor widow has put in more than all those who are contributing to the offering box. For they all contributed out of their abundance, but she out of her poverty has put in everything she had, all she had to live on'" (Mark 12:42–44).

day fifty

Job Description

Every house needs a grandmother in it.

Louisa May Alcott

The righteous flourish like the palm tree
and grow like a cedar in Lebanon.
They are planted in the house of the LORD;
they flourish in the courts of our God.
They still bear fruit in old age;
they are ever full of sap and green.

Psalm 92:12–14

"You're it!"

"How can that be? I'm not even playing!"

Suddenly I was roped into a rousing game of tag. I sauntered through the grassy yard, hoping to tag an unsuspecting grandchild. One eight-year-old grandson yelled, "Run, Grandma. Run."

"I don't run."

One of the cousins stopped and shouted in his direction, "She doesn't run!"

"You don't run?"

"Nope. I don't run."

Our grandchildren's ages span two decades. When the older grandkids were small, I ran! I ran a lot. Now I am a different person. Running around the backyard would not be a good idea.

Accepting the limitations that come with age is a difficult task. Slowing down takes us by surprise. We want to do the things we have always done. Or we want to live up to the expectations we have set for ourselves.

A friend confessed she was struggling with her role as grandma. Her sincere concern, "I don't like to bake."

There is no job description for grandmothers. Each grandmother's role is different.

Some grandmas bake. Some grandmas play games. Some grandmas babysit and do sleepovers. Other grandmas do crafts or teach grandchildren how to knit or sew. Some grandmas read books. Some grandmas go sledding. Some grandmas help with tuition or music lessons. Many grandmas sit, talk, and rock the babies. No grandma does it all.

There are grandmothers with severe limitations. For those grandmas, praying becomes a calling. Though they may not run, they do run to God with the concerns of family. Nothing is of greater value than that.

Comparing ourselves with others is always self-defeating. Creating a list of false expectations will only bring discouragement.

Accepting the way God made us and making peace with limitations release us to offer the best of ourselves to grandchildren. Every grandmother can contribute to the well-being of her grandchildren.

I think of grandmothering like making a deposit at the bank. The little things I do for the grandchildren are like going through the drive-through and making a deposit in their emotional and spiritual bank accounts. I ask the Lord to multiply my contribution and use it to encourage and strengthen them. Then I drive off and leave it in His hands.

Psalm 139:14 is a favorite for believers. We often consider this verse in terms of our physical being. But as we learn more about DNA, we realize our gifts and abilities are part of God's perfect plan as well. "I praise you, for I am fearfully and wonderfully made. Wonderful are your works; my soul knows it very well." God uses the unique gifts He placed in our DNA to serve our families. Some of us just don't have the baking gene.

A quote from Ralph Waldo Emerson encourages me as I nurture a relationship with my grandchildren. "Be silly. Be honest. Be kind." Each of these actions is like making a deposit in the bank and someday will pay relational dividends. We can trust the Lord to multiply our efforts.

When we are silly, honest, and kind in our grandchildren's presence, they don't care whether we run, do crafts, or bake. They simply enjoy our company.

Perhaps there is a grandmother job description. Here it is:

Be yourself. Trust the Lord.

Let us pray that . . .

- we will be content with where we are in life (Philippians 4:11).

- we will not lose heart as we recognize that God is at work in us in spite of increasing outward limitations (2 Corinthians 4:16).

- we will believe that the small things we do to nurture our grandchildren are not in vain (1 Corinthians 15:58).

- whatever we find to do, we will do it with all our hearts (Colossians 3:23).

- we will remember our prayers are the most precious gift of all (1 Thessalonians 5:16–17).

Heavenly Father, our grandchildren are our pride and joy. Thank you for each member of our family and for the love they bring. Lord, we desire to be used by you to serve our families. Remind us that we are not here to fix their problems or meet every need. Help us to wisely use our gifts and abilities to encourage and support where we are able. Give us gracious spirits as we accept our limitations and trust you. May we, like the righteous person in Psalm 92, bear fruit in old age. Amen.

Think and Do

- Do you occasionally find yourself doing things that are not your job? Attempting to fix grandkids' problems? Taking on a little too much responsibility? Worrying? Next time you are with your grandkids, try just having fun. Those are the moments they remember.

- Do you have a unique talent or hobby that you might share with an interested grandchild?
- Are you concerned that your unique deposits are not enough to make a difference in your grandchild's life? Read 2 Corinthians 9:8 and rejoice.

"Not that I am speaking of being in need, for I have learned in whatever situation I am to be content" (Philippians 4:11).

"We do not lose heart. Though our outer self is wasting away, our inner self is being renewed day by day" (2 Corinthians 4:16).

"Be steadfast, immovable, always abounding in the work of the Lord, knowing that in the Lord your labor is not in vain" (1 Corinthians 15:58).

"Whatever you do, work heartily, as for the Lord and not for men, knowing that from the Lord you will receive the inheritance as your reward. You are serving the Lord Christ" (Colossians 3:23–24).

"Rejoice always, pray without ceasing" (1 Thessalonians 5:16–17).

day fifty-one

Strengthen What Remains

The remedy for discouragement is the Word of God. When you feed your heart and mind with its truth, you regain your perspective and find renewed strength.

Warren Wiersbe

Wake up, and strengthen what remains and is about to die, for I have not found your works complete in the sight of my God.

Revelation 3:2

"You've had a stroke." No one wants to hear those words.

Many of us have watched loved ones struggle after receiving this diagnosis. Some fight to regain fluid speech. Many spend weeks in rehab to regain mobility. Others live with some level of permanent disability.

Fortunately, intensive physical, occupational, and speech therapies allow stroke victims to maximize their potential. While skilled therapists cannot repair the hurting brain, by focusing their work on strengthening what remains, quality of life is enhanced. A measure of independence (for some, complete independence) is restored.

The sooner the therapy begins, the better the outcome. The greater the patient's commitment to strengthening what remains, the more successful the recovery.

Strengthening what remains is the key.

These words came to mind recently. I was overwhelmed by national news. Openly lamenting the sad state of our world, I was complaining to God. It seemed our losses were piling up. The future seemed uncertain and scary.

As I poured out my misery over illness, crime, spiritual apathy, division, I confessed, "Lord, I don't know how to help."

Over the next few days, as I searched my Bible, my thoughts repeatedly returned to one verse in Revelation. "Wake up, and strengthen what remains and is about to die, for I have not found your works complete in the sight of my God" (3:2).

Wake up, and strengthen what remains.

This message was given to a particular church at a particular time about a particular situation. The church at Sardis (modern-day Turkey) had a reputation. While these believers bore the name Christian, their personal lives fell shockingly short of God's standards.

Their many works done in the name of Christ were incomplete. They lacked zeal. They were plagued by hypocrisy. The little that remained of their faith was like a flickering candle about to go out.

In spite of all that, verse 4 tells us that there was hope. In the midst of hypocrisy and sin, there were still faithful believers in the church at Sardis.

It was time to strengthen what remained.

While the command to strengthen what remains was given to the church at Sardis, there is application to our lives today.

In spite of some losses, there is much good that remains in today's church. We may not be able to bring radical, sweeping change, but we can certainly strengthen what remains. Like a physical therapist, working little by little to improve a patient's mobility or speech, we too can do the small, quiet work that will strengthen not only our churches, but our marriages, our homes, our grandchildren, our communities, our neighbors.

It takes determination and commitment. The sooner we get started, the better will be the outcome.

Strengthening what remains is a job we all can do.

We can strengthen our own faith through Bible study and prayer. "Faith comes from hearing, and hearing through the word of Christ" (Romans 10:17).

We can strengthen our own family through encouraging words. "Do not let any unwholesome talk come out of your mouths, but only what is helpful for building others up according to their needs, that it may benefit those who listen" (Ephesians 4:29 NIV).

We can strengthen our grandchildren through our prayers. "Pray without ceasing" (1 Thessalonians 5:17).

We can strengthen the church by actively stirring up the faith of fellow believers. "Let us consider how to stir up one another to love and good works, not neglecting to meet together, as is the habit of some, but encouraging one another, and all the more as you see the Day drawing near" (Hebrews 10:24–25).

Through generosity, we can strengthen the ministries that do the critical work of taking the gospel to the world. "Do not neglect to do good and to share what you have, for such sacrifices are pleasing to God" (Hebrews 13:16).

Strengthening what remains is a job for every Christian. Every Bible study, every prayer, every word of encouragement, every gift we give strengthens what remains.

The sooner we get started, the greater will be the outcome.

I pray God will multiply our efforts as we seek to strengthen the faith of family members, our churches, and our communities. I pray our grandchildren will reap the benefits of our commitment. May our grandchildren someday lead the charge to strengthen what remains.

Let us pray that . . .

- our grandchildren's faith will be strengthened, and they will walk in truth (3 John 1:4).

- our grandchildren's faith will be strong as they trust in Christ (Philippians 4:13).

- our grandchildren will find strength as they wait upon the Lord (Isaiah 40:31).

- our grandchildren will have the joy of the Lord and find strength in Him (Nehemiah 8:10).

- our grandchildren will be part of a community that intentionally stirs up and strengthens their faith (Hebrews 10:24–25).

- the Lord will guide us as we strengthen those who are faltering (1 Thessalonians 5:14).

Heavenly Father, we thank you for your Word and the way it ministers to us in our distress. We pray that you will help us in our own small ways to faithfully strengthen what remains of our own faith, the faith of our families, and the faith of fellow believers. May our words of encouragement and prayers be a source of strength to those we love. Make our churches strong in faith once again. We pray that you will send many believers into the lives of our precious grandchildren. May these Christians kindly and faithfully strengthen their faith. Amen.

Think and Do

- Read 1 Samuel 30:6. David was in distress. His family had been taken by the enemy. His own men were about to stone him. What did David do? Who took the initiative?

- Is there a particular ministry you feel called to strengthen? Does your church's children's ministry or another vital ministry need your financial, physical, or prayer support? Every small contribution is precious (Luke 21:3).

"I have no greater joy than to hear that my children are walking in the truth" (3 John 1:4).

"I can do all things through him who strengthens me" (Philippians 4:13).

"Even youths shall faint and be weary, and young men shall fall exhausted; but they who wait for the LORD shall renew their strength; they shall mount up with wings like eagles; they shall run and not be weary; they shall walk and not faint" (Isaiah 40:30–31).

"Do not be grieved, for the joy of the LORD is your strength" (Nehemiah 8:10).

"Let us consider how to stir up one another to love and good works, not neglecting to meet together, as is the habit of some, but encouraging one another, and all the more as you see the Day drawing near" (Hebrews 10:24–25).

"We urge you, brothers and sisters, warn those who are idle and disruptive, encourage the disheartened, help the weak, be patient with everyone" (1 Thessalonians 5:14 NIV).

day fifty-two

Jesus and the Ben Franklin Effect

The best way to destroy an enemy is to turn him into a friend.

Anonymous

Love your enemies, and do good, and lend, expecting nothing in return, and your reward will be great, and you will be sons of the Most High.

Luke 6:35

There was little reason to believe Ben Franklin would become a world leader, author, inventor, entrepreneur, or statesman. His education ended at the age of ten.

On his own, Franklin began an ambitious program of self-improvement. Borrowed books and debates with friends at the local taverns provided his curriculum, classrooms, and teachers.

One of the keys to Franklin's success was his understanding of human nature. Through careful observation, he acquired and polished his people skills. He was outgoing and friendly. He was also persuasive and cunning.

When he ran for a low-level clerk position, his opponent delivered a scathing speech. In spite of this, Franklin won the election. The memory of the stinging comments of his opponent gnawed at him.

Franklin was convinced he could turn this enemy into a friend. He wrote a letter to his opponent. Could he borrow a rare book from the man's library? The gentleman agreed. One week later, Franklin returned the book with a gracious thank-you note.

Franklin believed that when an individual does a kindness for you, it alters how they see you. He believed it was more effective than being the one doing the favor. Psychologists have named this principle the Ben Franklin Effect.

The next time Ben encountered this man, they greeted each other warmly. This began a lifelong friendship.

Ben Franklin was correct. But his philosophy is actually the Jesus effect. In the teachings of Jesus, we are commanded to do favors for those we don't like; we are asked to offer kindness to our enemies.

The result is a change in our feelings toward our foe. When we offer a kindness or receive a kindness, drama is replaced with empathy. We see each other as Jesus does—as people in need of compassion and love.

Jesus gave specific instructions on how we are to relate to those who oppose us. "I say to you who hear, Love your enemies, do good to those who hate you, bless those who curse you, pray for those who abuse you" (Luke 6:27–28).

Love. Do Good. Bless. Pray. It works.

In Matthew 7:12, Jesus taught what we have come to know as the Golden Rule. "Whatever you wish that others would do to you, do also to them, for this is the Law and the Prophets."

If we were the enemy, how would we hope to be treated? Do that.

Helping children to respond with kindness (in normal situations) may alter their perception of and feelings toward other children. Can childhood enemies become friends? Sometimes they can. In childhood relationships where friction and tension are normal and occasionally occur, children can practice the teachings of Jesus and choose to show kindness.

However, caution must be used when teaching children to love their enemies. Expecting children to respond in kindness while being humiliated is risky, unrealistic, unhealthy, and dismissive of their pain. Bullying is serious. It requires great wisdom from parents and teachers. It is a source of heartache for the entire family, and intervention is often needed. Kids do not have the maturity to go it alone. It's important for children to be protected and to learn that they can choose their friends wisely. They need to know when it is time to walk away.

What can grandparents do for the bullied child? First, we support the parents in their efforts on behalf of their child. Second, we love, encourage, and pray for the hurting grandchild.

What do we do for the child who is struggling to manage normal friendships? The same. We love, encourage, and pray.

Healthy friendships are an important ingredient for a successful, enjoyable life.

My prayer is that as my grandchildren mature they will take the words of Jesus to heart. May they love, do good, bless, and pray for others. May they, like Ben Franklin, acquire the people skills that cultivate rich friendships. May they grow into adults who replace drama with kindness. We ask the Lord to fill each child's life with loving, caring, moral, and supportive friends.

Let us pray that . . .

- our grandchildren will mature and learn to love those considered enemies (Matthew 5:44).

- our grandchildren will learn to treat others the way they would like to be treated (Matthew 7:12).

- our grandchildren will learn to be of help to others, even those who may oppose them (Proverbs 25:21).

- our grandchildren will not seek revenge, but trust the Lord (Proverbs 20:22).

- our grandchildren will not rejoice over the troubles that plague their enemies (Proverbs 24:17).

- our grandchildren will learn to love friends and enemies alike (1 John 4:7).

- our grandchildren who are hurting will be supported, comforted, and cared for (Matthew 10:42).

Heavenly Father, we thank you that while we were still your enemies, Christ died for us. Help us to follow the example of Jesus and do good

to others. Help us to love those who have hurt us. Enable us to model forgiveness. Give our grandchildren ears to hear your teachings and hearts to obey. May they learn little by little to love, bless, do good, and pray. Help them to remember to treat others the way they themselves want to be treated. Put a hedge around them, and keep them safe. May Jesus become their dearest friend. Amen.

Think and Do

- Childhood is a wonderful time to cast a vision for the beauty of friendships. *The Other Side* by Jacqueline Woodson is the story of two little girls who would not allow differences to keep them from becoming friends. It would be a worthwhile addition to your library.
- What would happen if tomorrow every school bully started treating other people the way they wanted to be treated? Pray for your local schools and families.
- Make the Golden Rule a household rule.

"I say to you, Love your enemies and pray for those who persecute you" (Matthew 5:44).

"Whatever you wish that others would do to you, do also to them, for this is the Law and the Prophets" (Matthew 7:12).

"If your enemy is hungry, give him bread to eat, and if he is thirsty, give him water to drink, for you will heap burning coals on his head, and the LORD will reward you" (Proverbs 25:21–22).

"Do not say, 'I will repay evil'; wait for the LORD, and he will deliver you" (Proverbs 20:22).

"Do not rejoice when your enemy falls, and let not your heart be glad when he stumbles" (Proverbs 24:17).

"Beloved, let us love one another, for love is from God, and whoever loves has been born of God and knows God" (1 John 4:7).

"Whoever gives one of these little ones even a cup of cold water because he is a disciple, truly, I say to you, he will by no means lose his reward" (Matthew 10:42).

day fifty-three

A Fresh Start

No matter how hard the past, you can always begin again.

Jack Kornfield

The steadfast love of the LORD never ceases; his mercies never come to an end; they are new every morning; great is your faithfulness.

Lamentations 3:22–23

Hope. You can feel it on September mornings. You can see it standing on street corners in cities and towns. Children juggle book bags, show off new shoes, and squeal as they reunite with friends. Boys tell jokes. Girls giggle as they wait for the yellow school bus.

Parents, wearing hopeful expressions, hang back and observe their children. Maybe this year will be better. Will math finally make sense? Will new friendships be forged? Will there be fewer tears?

With kids safe on the bus, moms and dads turn toward home. They comfort themselves with one thought. A new school year is a fresh start.

Adults need fresh starts too. Boredom or frustration on a job can afflict any working person. Polishing the résumé, scanning job sites, the employee feels a twinge of hope. Maybe a fresh start is all that is needed for work to be enjoyable again.

Fresh starts are a necessity.

Jesus offers us more than a fresh start. He offers us a clean slate.

Imagine all your sins and failures staring at you from a small chalkboard on your student-sized desk. Now imagine the joy when Jesus leans over your desk and lovingly wipes the slate clean.

Fresh starts, new beginnings, and clean slates are the essence of our Christian life. We are the freest people in the world.

We are free because our sins are forgiven. "If we confess our sins, he is faithful and just to forgive us our sins and to cleanse us from all unrighteousness" (1 John 1:9). Jesus wipes the slate entirely clean—no lingering chalk dust.

We are free because we are spotless. "Though your sins are like scarlet, they shall be as white as snow" (Isaiah 1:18).

We are free because we are brand-new creations. "Therefore, if anyone is in Christ, he is a new creation. The old has passed away; behold, the new has come" (2 Corinthians 5:17). What a complete fresh start.

We are free because we can put behind us the past that drags us down. Past sins, failures, and heartaches no longer determine our future. "But one thing I do: forgetting what lies behind and straining forward to what lies ahead, I press on toward the goal for the prize of the upward call of God in Christ Jesus" (Philippians 3:13–14).

With the past behind, we set our sights on new places, with new goals, and new blessings.

The greatest fresh start still lies ahead.

When Lazarus died, Jesus promised Mary that her brother would have a fresh start. "Jesus said to her, 'I am the resurrection and the life. Whoever believes in me, though he die, yet shall he live'" (John 11:25).

Everyone needs a fresh start now and again. Grandmas included.

Wouldn't our souls sing with joy if our grandchildren experienced the hope, peace, and freedom that comes from a fresh start and clean slate with Jesus?

Let us pray our grandchildren will experience renewal. May we freely offer them fresh starts when it is most needed. That may be the best gift we will ever give them.

Let us pray that . . .

- our grandchildren will understand they can be new creations in Christ (2 Corinthians 5:17).

- our grandchildren will come to Jesus for a fresh start and forgiveness (1 John 1:9; Isaiah 1:18).

- our grandchildren will walk in newness of life (Romans 6:4).
- our grandchildren will successfully put the past behind them and focus on the prize (Philippians 3:13–14).
- our grandchildren will clothe themselves in the new self (Ephesians 4:24).
- our grandchildren will sing a new song to the Lord (Psalm 40:3).
- our grandchildren will embrace God's mercy every day (Lamentations 3:22–23).

Heavenly Father, you have given us a fresh start. You have given us a clean slate! We are new creations! Thank you for the fresh starts we receive every day with the sunrise. Thank you for forgiveness and freedom from the weight of the past. We pray our grandchildren will run to you when they need a clean slate. We pray they will know the joy and freedom it brings. May they never hesitate to come to you one more time for forgiveness and hope. We pray for our grandchildren who need a second chance in friendships, school, sports, and life. May caring adults help them to find the grace and freedom they need. You are the God of fresh starts, and we love you. Amen.

Think and Do

- Springtime and Easter both encourage us to think of fresh starts, new life, and resurrection. *'Twas the Morning of Easter* by Glenys Nellist is a beautifully illustrated, rhyming story of Easter morning. It uses the pattern and rhythm of *'Twas the Night Before Christmas*, making it memorable to children.
- Reflect on 2 Corinthians 5:17 and Romans 6:4. How have you experienced a "new" life since you came to Christ? How have you changed?

"Therefore, if anyone is in Christ, he is a new creation. The old has passed away; behold, the new has come" (2 Corinthians 5:17).

"If we confess our sins, he is faithful and just to forgive us our sins and to cleanse us from all unrighteousness" (1 John 1:9).

"Come now, let us reason together, says the LORD: though your sins are like scarlet, they shall be as white as snow; though they are red like crimson, they shall become like wool" (Isaiah 1:18).

"We were buried therefore with him by baptism into death, in order that, just as Christ was raised from the dead by the glory of the Father, we too might walk in newness of life" (Romans 6:4).

"One thing I do: forgetting what lies behind and straining forward to what lies ahead, I press on toward the goal for the prize of the upward call of God in Christ Jesus" (Philippians 3:13–14).

"Put on the new self, created after the likeness of God in true righteousness and holiness" (Ephesians 4:24).

"He put a new song in my mouth, a song of praise to our God. Many will see and fear, and put their trust in the LORD" (Psalm 40:3).

"The steadfast love of the LORD never ceases; his mercies never come to an end; they are new every morning; great is your faithfulness" (Lamentations 3:22–23).

day fifty-four

Taste and See

The gospel to me is simply irresistible.

Blaise Pascal

Oh, taste and see that the LORD is good! Blessed is the man who takes refuge in him!

Psalm 34:8

A white-haired usher greeted my sisters and me with a cheery, "Good morning, young ladies." Wrapping his massive hand around each of ours, he slipped us a cellophane-wrapped treat. The kindness of that gentleman and the sweet candy were my first "taste" of church. I liked it.

A few years later, as a new Christian, I had the sweet experience of standing around a piano with friends, singing hymns and worship choruses. The fellowship and worship were my second taste of church. I liked this even better.

Every introduction into Christianity was a sweet experience for me. Each new discovery just gave me a greater appetite for the truth. I was sold.

One of our grandchildren was hesitant as he transitioned to youth group. After much encouragement, he gave it a try. The moment he tasted the sweet fellowship, he was hooked.

In Psalm 34, David was fleeing Saul—again. He also became the target of an aggressive Philistine leader. With God's help, David escaped the clutches of both of his enemies. In gratitude, he lists in verses 4–8 all that God has done for him.

I sought the LORD, and he answered me
and delivered me from all my fears.
Those who look to him are radiant,
and their faces shall never be ashamed.
This poor man cried, and the LORD heard him
and saved him out of all his troubles.
The angel of the LORD encamps
around those who fear him, and delivers them.

Oh, *taste and see that the LORD is good*!
Blessed is the one who takes refuge in him. (emphasis
added)

David was saying, "I can tell you all about His goodness to me, but
you need to experience Him for yourself. Once you taste His goodness
and love, there will be no turning back."

We can tell our loved ones about God's love and the ways He has
personally rescued us. Yet isn't the ultimate goal for each to experience
God's goodness for themselves?

Isn't it the cry of our hearts for our grandchildren to taste and see
that the Lord is good?

Tasting is a willful action. Ask the parent of any toddler. How many
times have you said, "You won't know if you like it until you taste it"?

We can't force tasting. But we can set the table for an amazing feast.

When grandkids cuddle up close to hear a Bible story, they sense
our love for them and for God. We give them a taste of His goodness.

When they see us offering grace and mercy to someone who has
hurt us, they get a taste of God's mercy.

When they are on the receiving end of our generosity and patience,
the credibility of our faith grows, and they thirst to know more.

Hearing their names in prayer, they are introduced to a heavenly
Father who cares for them. They are captivated by His sweet love.

We don't need to be perfect. We just need to believe as David did,
that when we taste His mercy, we see and understand that the Lord is
good. A prayerful, loving Christian life makes the gospel irresistible
to hungry souls.

Our words are still important. Like David we need to proclaim all
that God has done for us. It is vital to be ready with a response for

their questions, "always being prepared to make a defense to anyone who asks you for a reason for the hope that is in you; yet do it with gentleness and respect" (1 Peter 3:15).

We cannot force anyone to taste of God's goodness. But we can send an invitation and then prepare a feast.

I pray my grandchildren will have many sweet experiences that will lead them to declare to others, "Taste and see that the LORD is good!" (Psalm 34:8).

Let us pray that . . .

- our grandchildren will taste God's goodness in His mercy (Psalm 23:6).
- our grandchildren will taste God's goodness in His generosity (Psalm 84:11).
- our grandchildren will taste God's goodness in His statutes (Psalm 119:68).
- our grandchildren will taste God's goodness in His protection (Nahum 1:7–8).
- our grandchildren will taste God's goodness in His love (Psalm 107:1).
- our grandchildren will taste God's goodness in His forgiveness (Psalm 86:5).
- our grandchildren will taste God's goodness in the giving of His Son (John 3:16).

Heavenly Father, we have tasted of your goodness and have been blessed. We thank you that your Word is like honey to our lips. We thank you for the sweet fellowship of believers. We ask, Lord, that you would lead our grandchildren to taste and see that you are good. May they be welcomed into a group of Christians that will create a thirst for you. May they find the sweet truth of your Word satisfying to their souls. Amen.

Think and Do

- What was your first sweet church experience? What enticed you to want more? Did someone's witness make Christianity irresistible for you? If so, what qualities did they display?
- Read Psalm 31:19 and James 1:17. What do these verses tell you about the source of all the good things in our lives? What do these verses teach us about God's goodness? How can you openly express gratitude for all the good God has done in your life?

"Surely goodness and mercy shall follow me all the days of my life, and I shall dwell in the house of the LORD forever" (Psalm 23:6).

"For the LORD God is a sun and shield; the LORD bestows favor and honor. No good thing does he withhold from those who walk uprightly" (Psalm 84:11).

"You are good and do good; teach me your statutes" (Psalm 119:68).

"The LORD is good, a stronghold in the day of trouble; he knows those who take refuge in him" (Nahum 1:7).

"Oh give thanks to the LORD, for he is good, for his steadfast love endures forever!" (Psalm 107:1).

"For you, O Lord, are good and forgiving, abounding in steadfast love to all who call upon you" (Psalm 86:5).

"For God so loved the world, that he gave his only Son, that whoever believes in him should not perish but have eternal life" (John 3:16).

day fifty-five

The Balm of Gilead

Christ is the Good Physician. There is no disease He cannot heal; no sin He cannot remove; no trouble He cannot help. He is the Balm of Gilead, the Great Physician who has never yet failed to heal all the spiritual maladies of every soul that has come unto Him in faith and prayer.

John H. Aughey

Heal me, O LORD, and I shall be healed; save me, and I shall be saved, for you are my praise.

Jeremiah 17:14

Lip balm. Shiny, sparkly, flavored, tinted, or medicinal, my granddaughters loved them all. Windy Chicago winters make this soothing salve a necessity. It protects, it comforts, it repairs.

Balms have been an essential part of healing for thousands of years. Balms for infections. Balms for wounds. Balms for fevers. Balms for whatever ails you.

Gilead was known for its medicinal balm. The sick traveled to Gilead, hoping the precious ointment would cure their diseases. Caravans carried the carefully prepared balm throughout the region (Genesis 37:25).

In the book of Jeremiah, we read of the sins of God's people. They rejected His law. They refused to repent. They engaged in idol worship. They were greedy and oppressive. They even sacrificed their children.

Every day was a parade of self-delusion, self-righteousness, and hypocrisy.

They were sick.

God's repeated offers of mercy were spurned. The coming judgment for their stubbornness and rebellion would bring much grief.

In Jeremiah 8:22, the prophet weeps and wails. He is overcome by the sinfulness, sickness, and hard-heartedness of God's people. In utter hopelessness he cries, "Is there no balm in Gilead? Is there no physician there? Why then is there no healing for the wound of my people?" (NIV).

Jeremiah realized there was no human remedy, no balm in the world—not even the treasured balm of Gilead—that could heal the corrosive sinfulness that plagued God's people. As long as they refused to repent and return, there would be no cure.

The only cure for God's people was repentance.

Many believe that the balm of Gilead in Jeremiah symbolizes the cure and healing that only Jesus can bring. Bible scholar and commentator Matthew Henry wrote, "The blood of Christ is balm in Gilead."[43]

Is there a balm in Gilead for you? For me? For our grandchildren? Is there healing? Is there a Physician who can soothe and restore our wounded souls?

Yes, there is. Jesus is His name. There is no sin so great that He cannot forgive. There is no pain so deep that He cannot comfort.

He is our balm in Gilead—our cure, our remedy, our solution, our Savior. He is the only antidote for the sin that poisons us. The simple words of the beautiful African American spiritual, "There Is a Balm in Gilead," offer comfort.

There is a Balm in Gilead to make the wounded whole;
There is a balm in Gilead to heal the sin-sick soul.[44]

I pray that my grandchildren will not waste their days seeking earthly cures or remedies for their spiritual disease. My prayer is that they will accept the healing balm of Christ that God offers to them. May this balm soothe, protect, heal, and repair their souls. May all their spiritual ills be cured by the Great Physician.

Let us pray that . . .

- our grandchildren will recognize Jesus as the only way to God (John 14:6).

- our grandchildren will understand there is salvation in no other name (Acts 4:12).

- our grandchildren will allow Jesus to bind their spiritual wounds (Psalm 147:3).

- our grandchildren will allow Jesus to heal all their soul's diseases and will praise His name (Psalm 103:3).

- our grandchildren will repent and return to God for healing (2 Chronicles 7:13–14).

- our grandchildren will come with humility to the Great Physician for healing (Mark 2:17).

Heavenly Father, we are sinful people in need of a cure. We thank you for Jesus, our balm in Gilead, our healer, our cure, our physician. Forgive us for turning to the world to soothe our pain. We pray our grandchildren will understand that Jesus is the only source of healing. Be their balm in Gilead. Amen.

Think and Do

- Read Mark 2. What prompted Jesus to say that only the sick need a physician? Who was included in the "sinner" category? How was the condition of the Pharisees similar to God's people in Jeremiah? What must we guard against in our own lives?

- Have you heard of boo-boo balm? This healing salve, made with only natural ingredients, is great for soothing your little one's inevitable scrapes and scratches. You can find online recipes for making your own boo-boo balm with your older grandchildren. What a great opportunity to remind them that Jesus is the Healer who can soothe every hurt.

- Psalm 139 teaches us that God knows everything about us. He even saw our unformed substance. Yet the psalmist ends with these words: "Search me, O God, and know my heart! Try me and know my thoughts! And see if there be any grievous way in me, and lead me in the way everlasting!" (vv. 23–24). Meditate on those verses and ask God to graciously reveal and heal any sickness in your soul.

"Jesus said to him, 'I am the way, and the truth, and the life. No one comes to the Father except through me" (John 14:6).

"There is salvation in no one else, for there is no other name under heaven given among men by which we must be saved" (Acts 4:12).

"He heals the brokenhearted and binds up their wounds" (Psalm 147:3).

"Bless the LORD, O my soul, and all that is within me, bless his holy name! Bless the LORD, O my soul, and forget not all his benefits, who forgives all your iniquity, who heals all your diseases, who redeems your life from the pit, who crowns you with steadfast love and mercy" (Psalm 103:1–4).

"When I shut up the heavens so that there is no rain, or command the locust to devour the land, or send pestilence among my people, if my people who are called by my name humble themselves, and pray and seek my face and turn from their wicked ways, then I will hear from heaven and will forgive their sin and heal their land" (2 Chronicles 7:13–14).

"When Jesus heard it, he said to them, 'Those who are well have no need of a physician, but those who are sick. I came not to call the righteous, but sinners'" (Mark 2:17).

day fifty-six

Small Enough

The world asks, what does a man own? Christ asks, how does he use it?

Andrew Murray

For his invisible attributes, namely, his eternal power and divine nature, have been clearly perceived, ever since the creation of the world, in the things that have been made. So they are without excuse.

Romans 1:20

Theodore Roosevelt loved nature. He purchased 155 acres on Long Island. The retreat, known as Sagamore, became the summer White House for the Roosevelts.

There is a frequently repeated story of a conversation between naturalist William Beebe and President Roosevelt. The friends would frequently conclude an evening at Sagamore by strolling the lawn. Gazing skyward, the pair located Pegasus and the Andromeda galaxy. Quietly, the friends pondered the vastness and majesty of the universe. The time of reflection would end with Roosevelt announcing, "Now I think we are small enough! Let's go to bed."[45]

Roosevelt possessed a practical, down-to-earth faith, nurtured by his Dutch Reformed and Presbyterian roots. We imagine this highly important man, humbled by the vastness of the universe, would echo the words of Psalm 19:1–4.

The heavens declare the glory of God,
and the sky above proclaims his handiwork.

Day to day pours out speech
    and night to night reveals knowledge.
There is no speech, nor are there words,
    whose voice is not heard.
Their voice goes out through all the earth,
    and their words to the end of the world.

Nature is a precious gift. It was given to us for our welfare, benefit, and enjoyment. Psalm 19 reminds us that it is God's way of making His invisible attributes known to man.

God reveals himself to us in His creation. There is no corner of the world where this message cannot be heard. This revelation goes on day after day and night after night. It requires no spoken words. It communicates in every language.

First and foremost, nature reveals God as the creator. It highlights His infinite power and sovereignty. The perfection of His creation, seen in the tiniest detail of a flower or in the immensity of the Grand Canyon, reveals His wisdom, provision, love, and care.

It reminds us that though we are small, He is mighty.

The heavens and the earth speak to every person, every day, every hour, and every moment to the ends of the earth. We can be confident creation is speaking to our grandchildren today.

In the past, children spent dozens of hours outside each week, playing, exploring, dreaming. Some childhood specialists link a lack of exposure to nature with an increase in behavioral disorders and anxiety.

Nature plays a key role in human flourishing. More importantly, it plays a pivotal role in nurturing the spiritual lives of children. Hiking, biking, campfires, collecting rocks, fishing, lying in the grass, chasing fireflies, building sandcastles on the beach, all provide endless opportunities to experience God in His creation.

Last night a storm rolled through the upper Midwest. It took our gazebo with it. The roar of the wind, the pounding of the rain, the flashes of lightning were the tiniest fractions of God's great power. This morning, wind whips through the rain-washed locust tree outside the window. The mystery of where the wind came from and where it is going is like the mystery of the working of God's Spirit. Tiny birds perch expectantly on the birdfeeder. Not one of them will fall without the Father's notice.

God speaks. He is not silent.

I am so thankful that creation reveals almighty God. I am thankful that the Creator speaks to my grandchildren every day and every night. I pray they will listen and learn from all that they observe. May they regard creation and find comfort in knowing that though they are small, God is almighty.

Let us pray that . . .

- our grandchildren will acknowledge God as creator (Revelation 4:11).

- our grandchildren will see and hear God speak through creation (Psalm 19:1–4).

- our grandchildren will clearly see God's attributes through natural revelation (Romans 1:20).

- our grandchildren will consider the wonders of creation and be humbled (Job 37:14).

- our grandchildren will accept their stewardship responsibility (Genesis 1:28; 2:15).

- our grandchildren will look at creation and realize the source of their strength is God (Psalm 121:1–2).

Heavenly Father, speak, Lord, speak! You are always present. You are never silent. Help our grandchildren to know you through your creation. Lift their thoughts to you as they lift their eyes heavenward. Delight their hearts with the tiniest of flowers, the song of the birds, or the croak of a bullfrog. May they experience your love, power, and beauty as they observe the exquisite work of your hands. May their hearts trust you as you reveal yourself to them. Amen.

Think and Do

- *This I Know: Seeing God in the World He Made,* by Clay Anderson helps children see God in the world around them. This beautifully illustrated book is suited for preschool and early elementary children.

- Is there a nature activity you enjoy? Perhaps you can include your grandchildren. If limitations make the outdoors difficult, house plants, nature videos, or books can be great conversation starters.

- Do you recall a time the Lord revealed himself to you in nature? Journal about that experience. It may be a great story to share with a grandchild while on a walk, enjoying a picnic, working in the garden, or even looking out a window at the falling snow.

"Worthy are you, our Lord and God, to receive glory and honor and power, for you created all things, and by your will they existed and were created" (Revelation 4:11).

"The heavens declare the glory of God, and the sky above proclaims his handiwork. Day to day pours out speech, and night to night reveals knowledge. There is no speech, nor are there words, whose voice is not heard. Their voice goes out through all the earth, and their words to the end of the world" (Psalm 19:1–4).

"For his invisible attributes, namely, his eternal power and divine nature, have been clearly perceived, ever since the creation of the world, in the things that have been made. So they are without excuse" (Romans 1:20).

"Hear this, O Job; stop and consider the wondrous works of God. Do you know how God lays his command upon them and causes the lightning of his cloud to shine? Do you know the balancings of the clouds, the wondrous works of him who is perfect in knowledge . . . ?" (Job 37:14–16).

"God blessed them. And God said to them, 'Be fruitful and multiply and fill the earth and subdue it, and have dominion over the fish of the sea and over the birds of the heavens and over every living thing that moves on the earth'" (Genesis 1:28).

"The LORD God took the man and put him in the garden of Eden to work it and keep it" (Genesis 2:15).

"I lift up my eyes to the hills. From where does my help come? My help comes from the LORD, who made heaven and earth" (Psalm 121:1–2).

day fifty-seven

Marvelous Faith

Only in a world where faith is difficult can faith exist.

Peter Kreeft

When the Son of Man comes, will he find faith on earth?

Luke 18:8

We are amazed by our nine grandchildren. We are in awe of their unique, God-given personalities. We are moved by their tender hearts and love for one another. We are astonished at their creativity. From the two-year-old to the twenty-five-year-old, we are delighted by who they are becoming.

We marvel at the gift of grandchildren. We marvel at the goodness of God in making these children part of our lives. The writer of Proverbs 17:6 was right: "Grandchildren are the crown of the aged."

You know that feeling—the feeling of amazement, wonder, and astonishment at your blessings?

The New Testament tells us that Jesus also marveled—twice.

Jesus walked the dusty road to Nazareth with His disciples. He was going home. On the Sabbath, He entered the familiar synagogue, most likely the synagogue of His youth. Years before, He may have sat there, alongside other Jewish boys, studying the Hebrew Scriptures.

You would expect the hometown synagogue to roll out the red carpet for His arrival. That didn't happen.

As He spoke, sharing the good news with His neighbors, many bitterly questioned His authority. "'Is not this the carpenter, the son of Mary and brother of James and Joses and Judas and Simon? And are not his sisters here with us?' And they took offense at him" (Mark 6:3).

Jesus responded,

> "A prophet is not without honor, except in his hometown and among his relatives and in his own household." And he could do no mighty work there, except that he laid his hands on a few sick people and healed them. *And he marveled because of their unbelief.* (vv. 4–6, emphasis added)

In the very place one would expect to find great faith, Jesus found an appalling lack of it.

These were God's chosen people. They knew the Law and the Prophets. They watched for the coming of the Messiah.

They had known Jesus and His family since His childhood. Surely they had seen His kindness, integrity, and humility.

From village to village, travelers carried news of the miracles of Jesus and His wise teaching. The people of Nazareth could not plead ignorance. It was astonishing that they did not believe. No wonder Jesus "marveled because of their unbelief."

Luke 7 recounts a second time Jesus marveled. Once again, the issue was faith.

A centurion heard of Jesus. One of his favored servants was desperately ill. The Roman had a relationship with some of the Jewish elders. He asked these men to appeal to Jesus for the healing of his servant.

The leaders came to Jesus. "'He is worthy to have you do this for him, for he loves our nation, and he is the one who built us our synagogue.' And Jesus went with them" (Luke 7:4–6).

The centurion sent friends to meet Jesus on the way. They relayed his humble message. "Lord, do not trouble yourself, for I am not worthy to have you come under my roof. . . . But say the word, and let my servant be healed" (vv. 6–7).

The centurion's message amazed Jesus. "When Jesus heard these things, he marveled at him, and turning to the crowd that followed him, said, 'I tell you, not even in Israel have I found such faith'" (v. 9).

What Jesus did not find in Israel, He found in a gentile.

The centurion had no reason to believe. He did not have the benefits of Jewish heritage and teachings. His daily occupation meant he heard from other soldiers harsh, hateful comments about the Jews. Yet he believed. Jesus found faith in the most unlikely of people.

No wonder Jesus marveled at his faith.

In Luke 18:8, Jesus asks a probing question after a parable encouraging persistence in prayer: "When the Son of Man comes, will he find faith on earth?"

Just imagine Jesus coming to us and marveling at our faith.

It is my hope that should the Lord return in my lifetime, He would find faith in our family. I pray that my grandchildren will have an unshakable faith. I pray they will take advantage of the blessings of God's Word, fellowship with other believers, and worship to grow a marvelous, God-honoring faith.

Let us pray that . . .

- our grandchildren will have faith that pleases God, believing He exists and rewards those who seek Him (Hebrews 11:6).

- our grandchildren will have faith that comes from hearing the word (Romans 10:17).

- our grandchildren will walk by faith and not by sight (2 Corinthians 5:7).

- our grandchildren will cry out to the Lord to increase their faith (Luke 17:5–6).

- our grandchildren will have a faith that overcomes troubles (1 John 5:4).

- our grandchildren will stand firm in the Christian faith (1 Corinthians 16:13).

- our grandchildren's faith will be found to be more precious than gold (1 Peter 1:7).

- when Jesus returns, He will find faith in the hearts of our grandchildren (Luke 18:8).

Heavenly Father, we marvel at your goodness toward us. Daily we are amazed by the outpouring of your love and mercy. We thank you for all that you offer to us to grow our faith. We pray, increase our faith. Grant our grandchildren eyes and hearts to see you at work in the world and in their own lives. Encourage their faith through your Word and promises. May they have a marvelous faith that glorifies you. When you come again, may you find faith in our families. Amen.

Think and Do

- In Luke 1:1–5, the apostles are challenged by Jesus's teaching on forgiveness. Aware of their own need, they plead, "Increase our faith!" Are you aware of an area in your life where you need the Lord to increase your faith? Finances? Family relationships? Obedience? Forgiveness? Fear? What help can you find in Romans 10:17?

- Alisa Childers has written a clear and convincing argument for historic Christianity in *Another Gospel?: A Lifelong Christian Seeks Truth in Response to Progressive Christianity*.

- Do your grandchildren have questions that are difficult to answer? *Case for Faith for Kids* by Lee Strobel will give children the tools to explore biblical truths that will strengthen their faith.

"Without faith it is impossible to please him, for whoever would draw near to God must believe that he exists and that he rewards those who seek him" (Hebrews 11:6).

"Faith comes from hearing, and hearing through the word of Christ" (Romans 10:17).

"We are always of good courage. We know that while we are at home in the body we are away from the Lord, for we walk by faith, not by sight" (2 Corinthians 5:6–7).

"The apostles said to the Lord, 'Increase our faith!' And the Lord said, 'If you had faith like a grain of mustard seed, you could say to this mulberry tree, "Be uprooted and planted in the sea," and it would obey you'" (Luke 17:5–6).

"For everyone who has been born of God overcomes the world. And this is the victory that has overcome the world—our faith" (1 John 5:4).

"Be watchful, stand firm in the faith, act like men, be strong" (1 Corinthians 16:13).

"These [trials] have come so that the proven genuineness of your faith—of greater worth than gold, which perishes even though refined by fire—may result in praise, glory and honor when Jesus Christ is revealed" (1 Peter 1:7 NIV).

"When the Son of Man comes, will he find faith on earth?" (Luke 18:8).

day fifty-eight

Check Your Taillights

> Only a disciple can make a disciple.
> A. W. Tozer

> Older women . . . are to teach what is good, and so train the young women to love their husbands and children, to be self-controlled, pure, working at home, kind, and submissive to their own husbands, that the word of God may not be reviled.
> Titus 2:3–5

It was a dark and foggy night. The speaker eased out of the church parking lot and onto a dark and unfamiliar road. The fog hung like a curtain, blocking her view of everything, even the yellow lines.

Panic washed over her. Would she be able to stay on the winding and strange road? Would she be able to avoid any oncoming cars? Would she ever find her way home?

Creeping along, fearful that she would not see what was ahead, she began to pray.

Just then, two tiny red lights shone faintly through the darkness ahead. Taillights!

If she kept her eyes on those taillights, and the driver ahead was able to safely navigate the road, she too would be safe. She just needed to focus on those taillights.

With great relief, she arrived home safely, thanks to an unknown driver. Her prayers had been answered by a set of taillights.

God has often answered my prayers with taillights.

In a church kitchen in Indiana, I dried dishes and listened as older women talked of home and family. Their influence shaped my beliefs about marriage and family.

As a young mother with a sleepless baby, I needed taillights and knew it. As often as I could, I observed other moms. Their kindness and firmness with their children lit the way through my mist of confusion.

A young pastor at our first church spoke often of praying through Scripture. His example continues to light the way as I learn more about prayer.

My life has been blessed with a parade of taillights. They often guided me through the fog. Sometimes the lights drew me back to the path after I foolishly veered from the road.

In Philippians 3:17, Paul affirms this idea of Christians looking to others for encouragement and guidance in the faith. "Brothers, join in imitating me, and keep your eyes on those who walk according to the example you have in us." In 1 Corinthians 11:1 he informs believers of why they should imitate him. "Be imitators of me, as I am of Christ."

The familiar passage of Titus 2 reminds older women they have a responsibility to be taillights for young women. "Older women . . . are to teach what is good" (v. 3). Women have a unique privilege of lighting the way for one another.

From time to time, we need to check our own taillights for burned-out bulbs, cracks, or grime that would dim the glow. Unbeknownst to us, someone may be watching our taillights.

It has been over forty years ago that my husband and I invited a nine-year-old Kathy to our home for Sunday dinner. We ate, did a craft, played a game, baked cookies. It was a simple, quiet, restful afternoon.

A few years ago, we received a touching note from Kathy. She thanked us for that Sunday afternoon nearly four decades ago. She wrote that the time we spent together influenced her life. We were speechless. We had no idea that such a simple gesture could mean so much.

It is an honor to lead, guide, and light the way for younger believers on their spiritual journeys. We should do so with humility and care. The disciplines of Bible study and prayer will keep our taillights clean and in good repair.

I pray that a parade of godly people will light the way for each of my grandchildren. May their lives be filled with believers who imitate Christ. I pray loving believers will guide them through the fog and inspire them to follow Jesus more closely.

Let us pray that . . .

- our grandchildren will follow the examples of those who show good works, integrity, and dignity (Titus 2:7).
- our grandchildren will have discernment in whom they follow (1 Peter 5:1–4).
- our grandchildren will imitate those who imitate Christ (1 Corinthians 11:1).
- our grandchildren will focus their eyes on those who live godly lives (Philippians 3:17).
- we will let our light shine and be an example to younger believers (Matthew 5:16; Titus 2:3–5).

Heavenly Father, we are grateful for those who have gone before us and been such faithful examples. Help us to live in such a way that we can guide others through the fog. May our grandchildren look for godly people to light their way. Help them to be wise as they choose whom to follow. May their guides be imitators of Jesus and provide a steady light through the dark. Amen.

Think and Do

- Whose taillights have you followed? Have you thanked them?
- Does your church have a mentor ministry? If not, can you find an informal way to be a spiritual encouragement to younger believers? Try sending a note, sharing a coffee, or even asking for prayer requests. Simple connections communicate so much.

- Read Philippians 3:17 again. Is there a mature Christian who is lighting your way today? What does it mean for you to keep your eyes on those who are imitating Christ?

"Show yourself in all respects to be a model of good works, and in your teaching show integrity, dignity" (Titus 2:7).

"I exhort the elders among you, as a fellow elder and a witness of the sufferings of Christ, as well as a partaker in the glory that is going to be revealed: shepherd the flock of God that is among you, exercising oversight, not under compulsion, but willingly, as God would have you; not for shameful gain, but eagerly; not domineering over those in your charge, but being examples to the flock. And when the chief Shepherd appears, you will receive the unfading crown of glory" (1 Peter 5:1–4).

"Be imitators of me, as I am of Christ" (1 Corinthians 11:1).

"Join in imitating me, and keep your eyes on those who walk according to the example you have in us" (Philippians 3:17).

"In the same way, let your light shine before others, so that they may see your good works and give glory to your Father who is in heaven" (Matthew 5:16).

"Older women likewise are to be reverent in behavior, not slanderers or slaves to much wine. They are to teach what is good, and so train the young women to love their husbands and children, to be self-controlled, pure, working at home, kind, and submissive to their own husbands, that the word of God may not be reviled" (Titus 2:3–5).

day fifty-nine

Run Your Race

God knows our situation; He will not judge us as if we had no difficulties to overcome. What matters is the sincerity and perseverance of our will to overcome them.

C. S. Lewis

I have fought the good fight, I have finished the race, I have kept the faith.

2 Timothy 4:7

Just before the Olympic decathlon event, Jim Thorpe's shoes were missing. His teammate had one spare shoe he could borrow, and the second shoe he found by rummaging through a trash can. The determined athlete had two shoes of different sizes. To make the larger one fit, he wore an extra sock.

This glitch in footwear threatened to ruin his chances in the upcoming events. It could have ended his career. But it didn't.

That day, wearing someone else's shoes and mismatched socks, Jim won the high jump and the 110-meter hurdle. The next day, still in ill-fitting footwear, he ran the 1,500 meter in 4 minutes and 40.1 seconds.

He overcame a challenge in spectacular fashion. What many would see as an unfair disadvantage didn't deter Jim Thorpe from his goal. He never gave up.

At the 1912 Olympics in Sweden, King Gustav slipped a gold medal around Jim's neck and told him he was the greatest athlete in the world.[46]

Scripture commands us to persevere in our faith even when facing life's trials. We are to persevere even when life seems unfair. We persist in our faith, not to win Olympic gold but to win something more precious. "Blessed is the one who perseveres under trial because, having stood the test, that person will receive the crown of life that the Lord has promised to those who love him" (James 1:12 NIV).

Our prize is more precious than gold and is promised to us by Jesus himself.

Paul uses running a race as an illustration of persevering in faith. He encourages the Corinthians to run. "Do you not know that in a race all the runners run, but only one receives the prize? So run that you may obtain it" (1 Corinthians 9:24).

The book of Hebrews picks up the idea of persevering in faith as running a race. "Let us run with perseverance the race marked out for us" (12:1 NIV).

We each have a race marked out for us. The path is sometimes smooth and sometimes treacherous. Some of us have been running for a long time. We still have a ways to go. Most of us are tired. More than once we have considered giving up because of the obstacles and trials. We would like to linger at an aid station with a water bottle and take a break. Maybe it is time for us to throw off what weighs us down, tighten our laces, and hit the track.

The writer of Hebrews gives us a focus for our running that gives us courage to go on: "fixing your eyes on Jesus, the pioneer and perfecter of faith" (v. 2 NIV). Keeping our eyes on Jesus, we are inspired and encouraged. When we think of Him standing at the finish line, cheering us on, we find strength to persevere.

Jesus ran the race set before Him. He made it to the finish line. Completing His unique race brought Him joy and honor. He ran it for us. He will help us to finish our own race.

Jim Thorpe's race to gold was rocky in many ways. By keeping his eye on the prize, refusing to be a victim or to throw in the towel, he made it to the finish line in glorious fashion.

I know that my grandchildren's race will have its share of challenges and pitfalls. I pray they will run for the prize that Jesus promises. I pray they will overcome life's challenges in spectacular fashion by persevering and trusting Jesus to get them to the finish.

"I can do all things through him who strengthens me" (Philippians 4:13).

Let us pray that . . .

- our grandchildren will not give up in doing good (Galatians 6:9).
- our grandchildren will remain firm in the faith (1 Corinthians 16:13).
- our grandchildren will run to win the prize (1 Corinthians 9:24).
- our grandchildren will know that God is with them in their trials (Joshua 1:9).
- our grandchildren will rely on God to strengthen and help them (Isaiah 40:30–31).
- our grandchildren will fix their eyes on Jesus as they run with perseverance the race before them (Hebrews 12:1–2).

Heavenly Father, we thank you for the example of perseverance we see in Jesus. Lord, we pray that our grandchildren will develop perseverance in life. We pray they will sense your presence all along the course toward the finish line. May they throw off anything that would weigh them down. Give them hope and resilience even when life is unfair. May our grandchildren run their race and receive the crown of life promised to those who love Jesus. Amen.

Think and Do

- *Brave Young Knight* by Karen Kingsbury is a children's book that tells the story of a little boy who persevered in doing what was right. This story will get your grandchildren thinking about their own choices.
- Nearly 35,000 runners participated in the 2021 Chicago Marathon. Many wondered if they would make it to the finish line. Fortunately, the crowds and event planners lining a difficult section

gave them the energy to complete their race. Read and reflect on Hebrews 12:1. What factor provides motivation for us to finish our race? Who is cheering you on? What two things are we to do in order to make it to the finish line? Pray that the Lord will help you persevere.

"Let us not grow weary of doing good, for in due season we will reap, if we do not give up" (Galatians 6:9).

"Be watchful, stand firm in the faith, act like men, be strong" (1 Corinthians 16:13).

"Do you not know that in a race all the runners run, but only one receives the prize? So run that you may obtain it" (1 Corinthians 9:24).

"Have I not commanded you? Be strong and courageous. Do not be frightened, and do not be dismayed, for the LORD your God is with you wherever you go" (Joshua 1:9).

"Even youths shall faint and be weary, and young men shall fall exhausted; but they who wait for the LORD shall renew their strength; they shall mount up with wings like eagles; they shall run and not be weary; they shall walk and not faint" (Isaiah 40:30–31).

"Therefore, since we are surrounded by so great a cloud of witnesses, let us also lay aside every weight, and sin which clings so closely, and let us run with endurance the race that is set before us, looking to Jesus, the founder and perfecter of our faith, who for the joy that was set before him endured the cross, despising the shame, and is seated at the right hand of the throne of God" (Hebrews 12:1–2).

day sixty

Laus Deo

What is the chief end of man?
Man's chief end is to glorify God and to enjoy him forever.

Westminster Shorter Catechism

Fear God and keep his commandments, for this is the whole duty of man.

Ecclesiastes 12:13

An impressive marble obelisk, the towering Washington Monument stands as a memorial and expression of gratitude to the first president of the United States.

The project was plagued by repeated delays in funding and construction. When completed in 1885, it stood 555 feet, 5⅛ inches tall. At that time, it was the tallest building in the world. Today the Washington Monument continues to be the tallest building in our nation's capital.

On December 6, 1884, an aluminum capstone was set on the very top of the structure. The metal was chosen because of its resilience and resistance to tarnishing. The capstone would shield the pinnacle from damaging rain and lightning. Casting an aluminum pyramid of this size was an engineering accomplishment.

When in place, the capstone pointed heavenward and bore a Latin inscription.

Laus Deo. Praise be to God.

A capstone is normally an architectural term. It also can be defined as a crowning achievement. Placing the aluminum pyramid and inscription on the top of the monument was the crowning achievement of the architects, engineers, and craftsmen.

As believers, the crowning achievement of our lives, the capstone, is summed up in *The Westminster Shorter Catechism.* "What is the chief end of man? Man's chief end is to glorify God and to enjoy him forever."[47]

We—grandparents and grandchildren alike—were made to glorify God.

Glorifying God is our highest calling, the pinnacle of our existence. Isaiah understood that as he wrote down what God said about the future gathering of people from all nations. This group would be made up of "everyone who is called by my name, whom I created for my glory, whom I formed and made" (Isaiah 43:7).

We were made for God's glory.

Scripture is filled with expressions of praise and commands to glorify God. The psalmist, in spite of the rejection of his peers wrote, "My mouth is filled with your praise, and with your glory all the day" (Psalm 71:8). Every day, he glorified God.

In an emotional expression of praise, the writer of 1 Chronicles pens this beautiful passage. "Ascribe to the LORD, O families of the peoples, ascribe to the LORD glory and strength! Ascribe to the LORD the glory due his name; bring an offering and come before him! Worship the LORD in the splendor of holiness" (16:28–29).

We were made to glorify God. When we do, we are constructing a monument to His goodness, grace, and holiness.

The chief end of man is to glorify God, *and* to enjoy Him forever.

We—grandparents and grandchildren alike—were created to enjoy God.

Psalm 16, possibly written during a time of crisis, gives us a picture of David enjoying God even in perilous times. "You make known to me the path of life; in your presence there is fullness of joy; at your right hand are pleasures forevermore" (v. 11).

David experienced intellectual, emotional, and spiritual joy in God's presence. The shepherd, warrior, and king found fullness of joy in his

God. His relationship with God filled him with a pleasure that would continue forever.

David relished and enjoyed God's words. "In the way of your testimonies I delight as much as in all riches" (119:14). David delighted in God himself. "Delight yourself in the LORD, and he will give you the desires of your heart" (37:4).

Even those who are famished, thirsty, and empty can find satisfaction in their relationship with God. "For he satisfies the longing soul, and the hungry soul he fills with good things" (107:9).

Our fullness of joy is not for our earthly life alone. We will enjoy Him forever.

When addressing the persecution that would be faced by believers, Jesus encouraged His followers to rejoice on those days, because of the future promise of heaven. "Rejoice in that day, and leap for joy, for behold, your reward is great in heaven" (Luke 6:23).

The crowning achievement of our lives, the capstone, is to glorify God and enjoy Him forever.

Let us pray that this also will be the crowning achievement of our grandchildren's lives. May glorifying God be the focus of their days. May they discover in God's presence fullness of joy forevermore.

Laus Deo.

Let us pray that . . .

- our grandchildren will know that they were created for God's glory (Isaiah 43:6–7).

- our grandchildren will give God the glory due His name (Psalm 29:1–2).

- our grandchildren will know that glory belongs to God alone (Psalm 86:12).

- our grandchildren will glorify God in everything that they do (1 Corinthians 10:31).

- our grandchildren will find joy and satisfaction in their salvation (Habakkuk 3:18).

- our grandchildren will learn to delight in God (Psalm 37:4).

- our grandchildren will look forward to enjoying their reward in heaven (Luke 6:23).
- our grandchildren's hearts will be satisfied in God continually (Isaiah 58:11).

Heavenly Father, regardless of our age, our purpose remains the same—to bring glory to you. We long for the crowning achievement of our lives to be this: Glorifying and enjoying you forever. Grant us undivided hearts and perseverance. Lord, you know how dearly we love our grandchildren. We do not ask that they would be given riches or lives of ease. We ask instead that their lives would overflow with purpose and meaning. May they find in your presence fullness of joy. May they glorify and praise you every day. When they reach our ages, may it be said that the crowning achievement of their lives was glorifying and enjoying you. Amen.

Think and Do

- Read and meditate on the beautiful words of Psalm 73:23–26, 28. The psalmist exudes joy as he describes his relationship with God. What phrases speak to your heart?
- To know God is to love and enjoy Him. *I Am Devotional: 100 Devotions About the Names of God* by Diane Stortz will help your grandchildren develop a strong faith that can become the crowning achievement of their lives.

"I will say to the north, Give up, and to the south, Do not withhold; bring my sons from afar and my daughters from the end of the earth, everyone who is called by my name, whom I created for my glory, whom I formed and made" (Isaiah 43:6–7).

"Ascribe to the LORD, O heavenly beings, ascribe to the LORD glory and strength. Ascribe to the LORD the glory due his name; worship the LORD in the splendor of holiness" (Psalm 29:1–2).

"I give thanks to you, O Lord my God, with my whole heart, and I will glorify your name forever" (Psalm 86:12).

"Whether you eat or drink, or whatever you do, do all to the glory of God" (1 Corinthians 10:31).

"Though the fig tree should not blossom, nor fruit be on the vines, the produce of the olive fail and the fields yield no food, the flock be cut off from the fold and there be no herd in the stalls, yet I will rejoice in the LORD; I will take joy in the God of my salvation" (Habakkuk 3:17–18).

"Delight yourself in the LORD, and he will give you the desires of your heart" (Psalm 37:4).

"Rejoice in that day, and leap for joy, for behold, your reward is great in heaven; for so their fathers did to the prophets" (Luke 6:23).

"The LORD will guide you continually and satisfy your desire in scorched places and make your bones strong; and you shall be like a watered garden, like a spring of water, whose waters do not fail" (Isaiah 58:11).

Notes

1. Dan Scherillo, "Salt and Light" (sermon, Parkside Church, Chagrin Falls, OH, November 4, 2018), https://www.parksidechurch.com/learn/resources/media-center/sermon/salt-and-light/.

2. Grant Richison, "1 Peter 5:7," Verse-by-Verse Commentary, February 1, 1998, https://versebyversecommentary.com/1998/02/01/1-peter-57/.

3. Andy Stanley, *The Best Question Ever* (Colorado Springs: Multnomah, 2004).

4. *The Repair Shop*, BBC One, 2017–2021, https://www.bbc.co.uk/programmes/b08l581p.

5. Christopher Klein, "The Two Mothers Who Molded Lincoln," History, August 29, 2018, https://www.history.com/news/the-two-mothers-who-molded-lincoln.

6. C. S. Lewis, *Letters of C. S. Lewis*, rev. ed., edited and with a memoir by W. H. Lewis, ed. Walter Hooper (San Francisco: HarperOne, 2017), 651.

7. Matthew Henry, *Zondervan NIV Matthew Henry Commentary* (Grand Rapids, MI: Zondervan, 2010), notes to Zechariah 12:9–14.

8. Fyodor Dostoyevsky, *Notes from Underground, and the Grand Inquisitor* (New York: Dutton, 1960), 84.

9. "Billy Graham's Father and the Prayer Heard Around the World," Billy Graham Evangelistic Association, May 29, 2018. https://billygraham.org/story/billy-grahams-father-prayer-heard-around-world/.

10. Elisabeth Elliot, *Through Gates of Splendor* (Wheaton, IL: Tyndale, 1986), 3.

11. Tertullian, *Apology and De Spectaculis*, trans. T. R. Glover (Cambridge, MA: Harvard University Press, 1998), 49.

12. Michael Green, "Unaware of His Own Possessions," Ministry127, accessed October 15, 2021, https://ministry127.com/resources/illustration/unaware-of-his-possessions.

13. Aleksandr Solzhenitsyn, *The Gulag Archipelago, 1918–1956*, vol. 2, trans. Thomas P. Whitney (New York: Harper Perennial Modern Classics, 2007), 616.

14. Johann Wolfgang von Goethe, *A Dictionary of Thoughts: Being a Cyclopedia of Laconic Questions from the Best Authors of the World, Both Ancient and Modern*, ed. Tryon Edwards (Detroit: F. B. Dickerson, 1908), 277.

15. "The 50 Countries Where It's Most Dangerous to Follow Jesus in 2021," CT Editors, January 13, 2021, https://www.christianitytoday.com /news/2021/january/christian-persecution-2021-countries-open-doors -watch-list.html.

16. Søren Kierkegaard, "Followers, Not Admirers," in *Bread and Wine: Readings for Lent and Easter* (Walden, NY: Plough, 2003), 60.

17. E. M. Bounds, *Purpose in Prayer* (New Kensington, PA: Whitaker House, 1997).

18. "The Declaration of Christmas Peace," Turku, https://www.turku .fi/en/christmas-city/declaration-christmas-peace.

19. Larry Crabb, *The Safest Place on Earth* (Nashville: W Publishing, 1999).

20. *Merriam-Webster*, s.v. "fret (v.)," https://www.merriam-webster.com /dictionary/fret.

21. Paul Tripp, "The Ultimate Cataclysmic Psalm," May 29, 2020, https://www.paultripp.com/articles/posts/the-ultimate-cataclysmic-psalm.

22. Max Lucado, *Facing Your Giants: A David & Goliath Story for Everyday People* (Nashville: Thomas Nelson, 2006), 130.

23. "Charitable Giving Showed Solid Growth, Climbing to $449.64 Billion in 2019," Giving USA, June 16, 2020, https://givingusa.org/giving -usa-2020-charitable-giving-showed-solid-growth-climbing-to-449-64 -billion-in-2019-one-of-the-highest-years-for-giving-on.

24. Greg Lukianoff and Jonathan Haidt, *The Coddling of the American Mind* (New York: Penguin, 2018), 55.

25. Seth Hammond, "Why Did Jesus Weep over Jerusalem?" Christ Covenant PCA, April 6, 2020, https://www.christcov.org/seths-soundbites /post/why-did-jesus-weep-over-jerusalem.

26. James Gordon Meek et al., "Kayla Mueller in Captivity," ABC News, August 25, 2016, https://abcnews.go.com/International/kayla -mueller-captivity-courage-selflessness-defended-christian-faith/story ?id=41626763.

27. Anna Brand, "A Letter From Kayla Mueller: 'I will not give in,'" MSNBC, February 10, 2015, https://www.msnbc.com/msnbc/letter -kayla-mueller-american-hostage-isis-i-will-not-give-in-msna525881.

28. Blue Letter Bible, s.v. "kamptō," accessed October 15, 2021, https:// www.blueletterbible.org/lexicon/g2578/kjv/tr/0-1/.

29. Online Etymology Dictionary, s.v. "adoption," accessed October 4, 2021, https://www.etymonline.com/search?q=adoption.

30. Billy Graham and Max Lucado, *God's Blessing for You* (Nashville: Thomas Nelson, 2007), 29.

31. C. S. Lewis, *Letters of C. S. Lewis*, rev. ed., ed. and with a memoir by W. H. Lewis (Orlando: Harcourt, 1993), 395.

32. Gladys Hunt, *Honey for a Child's Heart*, 4th ed. (Grand Rapids, MI: Zondervan, 2002), 23.

33. Sarah Clarkson, *Caught Up in a Story* (Monument, CO: Storyformed Books, 2013), 29.

34. Gary Thomas, *Cherish: The One Word that Changes Everything for Your Marriage* (Grand Rapids, MI: Zondervan, 2017), 18.

35. USAFacts, "The State of American Households: Smaller, More Diverse and Unmarried," *U.S. News & World Report*, February 14, 2020, https://www.usnews.com/news/elections/articles/2020-02-14/the-state-of-american-households-smaller-more-diverse-and-unmarried.

36. "The Story Behind the Hymn 'Rock of Ages,'" The Tabernacle Choir Blog, March 10, 2015, https://www.thetabernaclechoir.org/articles/rock-of-ages-history.html.

37. Augustus Toplady, quoted in Chris Fenner, "Rock of Ages, Cleft for Me," Hymnology Archive, April 26, 2019, https://www.hymnologyarchive.com/rock-of-ages-cleft-for-me.

38. C. S. Lewis, *A Grief Observed* (San Francisco: HarperOne, 1961), 11.

39. Donne Davis, *When Being a Grandma Isn't So Grand: 4 Keys to L.O.V.E. Your Grandchild's Parents* (self-pub., Lulu.com, 2012), xvi.

40. *Merriam-Webster*, s.v. "acknowledge," accessed October 18, 2021, https://www.merriam-webster.com/dictionary/acknowledge.

41. Caroline Davies, "'Spend, Spend, Spend' Football Pools Winner, Viv Nicholson, Dies Aged 79," *Guardian*, April 12, 2015, https://www.theguardian.com/uk-news/2015/apr/12/spend-spend-spend-football-pools-winner-viv-nicholson-dies-aged-79.

42. Jan Silvious, "Give me neither poverty nor riches . . . ," Facebook video, June 8, 2021, https://www.facebook.com/jan.silvious.1/videos/1700564816997974.

43. Matthew Henry, *Matthew Henry's Commentary on the Whole Bible: Volume IV-II, Jeremiah to Lamentations*, ed. Anthony Uyl (Woodstock, ON: Devoted Publishing, 2017), 64.

44. H. T. Burleigh, "Balm in Gilead" (New York: G. Ricordi & Co., 1919), https://www.okcu.edu/uploads/music/docs/Balm-in-Gilead-Low-Key.pdf.

45. "Now We Are Small Enough," Bible.org, February 2, 2009, https://bible.org/illustration/now-we-are-small-enough.

46. Sally Jenkins, "Why Are Jim Thorpe's Olympic Records Still Not Recognized?," *Smithsonian Magazine*, July 2012, https://www.smithsonianmag.com/history/why-are-jim-thorpes-olympic-records-still-not-recognized-130986336/; Bob Wheeler, "Jim Thorpe: World's Greatest Athlete," YouTube, August 24, 2012, https://www.youtube.com/watch?v=MHu_UdqCZDs&t=1513s.

47. G. I. Williamson, *The Westminster Shorter Catechism: For Study Classes*, 2nd ed. (Phillipsburg, NJ: P&R, 2003), 1.

Help us get the word out!

Our Daily Bread Publishing exists to feed the soul with the Word of God.

If you appreciated this book, please let others know.

- Pick up another copy to give as a gift.
- Share a link to the book or mention it on social media.
- Write a review on your blog, on a bookseller's website, or at our own site (odb.org/store).
- Recommend this book for your church, book club, or small group.

Connect with us:

f @ourdailybread

◎ @ourdailybread

🐦 @ourdailybread

Our Daily Bread Publishing
PO Box 3566
Grand Rapids, Michigan 49501 USA

✉ books@odb.org